WHO ARE YOU,

A HELPER OR A SERVANT?

Fifty-five differences between a helper and a servant

Bimbo Sagbola

Published by Sycamore Consult Ltd

London, England

ISBN 978-0-9933820

TABLE OF CONTENTS

PREFACE

The vision for this book was born out of the desire to share my experience serving the LORD in various capacities over the last 30 years. It is my hope that this book will help men and women around the world serving in their local churches, or even in their secular jobs, to understand what the differences are between just serving and serving God without holding back.

We all at some point may have heard this sentence before: ***"It is better to learn from other people's mistakes than to learn from your own".*** You are better off watching someone else make errors, and using them as a yard stick to measure your own journey of life.

It is an understatement to say that many mistakes were made in those thirty years. Some of such mistakes were down to naivety, or the lack of deep understanding and knowledge of what was expected of a servant. This does means that I have had to rise and fall on several occasions, and learn from countless errors. I also observed how others have made life changing decisions, some of which appeared right at the time.

As I became more spiritually matured, with more revelation of the Word, I came to realise how wrong these actions were. I have seen many people over the years physically, emotionally, morally and spiritually handicapped by such errors and never recover.

My wish for you as you read this book is to come to a good understanding of what is required of you as a servant of our Lord Jesus Christ. This book will not only educate you as you continue to serve the Lord, but it will also empower you in your business, in your daily job and in all areas of your life.

ACKNOWLEDGEMENTS

I give glory to God for His grace and for giving me the opportunity and the privilege to serve and know Him. He has been my rock, my strength and my source of inspiration through my journey of life.

My sincere appreciation goes to my mentors, motivators, the shepherds and the prophets over me, Pastor Matthew Ashimolowo and Pastor (Mrs) Yemisi Ashimolowo who trusted in me and gave me the opportunity to serve in various leadership roles over the years.

I cannot forget the hours of labour put into the editing of the manuscript by Ola Obafisoye, and Mr & Mrs Aremu. How could I forget The Big Give Back team particularly Dr Elizabeth Babatunde and David Clarke who worked tirelessly with me to make this book a reality. You are fantastic bunch.

I thank God for Moni Lanlehin who constantly reassured me by acknowledging the ability of God in me. And to Laetitia Kpenou and Chiedu Nwanze who gave a master touch to the book by formatting and designing the cover.

My reserved, deepest love and appreciation to my beautiful wife and help meet, Mojisola, and my two God given daughters, Tumininu and Olabisi who made lots of sacrifices to ensure this book became a reality. Your love, support and encouragement cannot be overemphasised. I love you all.

FOREWORD

Faithfulness and commitment are rare commodities these days. It seems as if everyone wants to assert their opinion, not minding if their opinion is the right or wrong one for the occasion.

True commitment is a necessity. Nothing works without it. No association achieves its goals, however lofty, and no relationship can be strong, unless the people involved are committed. Organisations will never advance and visions will not be achieved unless there is commitment.

Many times, I use the example of the typical English breakfast to explain the difference between involvement and commitment. The English breakfast contains eggs and bacon. To make this possible, a chicken has to lay an egg but a pig has to die to make the bacon. The chicken was involved but the pig was sacrificed. That is commitment.

Judas was involved with Jesus but he was not committed. Commitment is staying longer, picking up the cross and following.

Bimbo Sagbola's book has highlighted the virtues of serving with a heart of ultimate loyalty.

Loyalty goes the extra mile. It carries out the vision of the leader, sometimes before it is even verbalised. Loyalty covers the perceived weakness of the leader. It does not stop but makes sure the vision of the leader is promoted.

The contents of this book will help anyone who wants to serve with the right heart. This book also makes for a good training manual for effective discipleship.

Matthew Ashimolowo

INTRODUCTION

Romans 1:1

Paul, a servant of Christ Jesus, called to be an apostle and set apart for the gospel of God

In this scripture, the Bible referred to Paul as; **"a servant of Christ Jesus"**, not a helper for Christ Jesus. Paul is arguably the most honourable and exemplary servant in the Bible. He was not originally one of the twelve disciples and never really relates with Jesus Christ, neither was he educated or trained in the same "upper class school" as the disciples. Yet, he distinguished himself and stood out from the rest of the disciples. Before he met with the Lord and his conversion, Paul was persecuting Christians. He was working for his masters and not serving. Although he was said to be zealous, all his energy was mainly for his own gain and for his own selfish ends.

The word "serve" is derived from the word servant. Servant is mentioned in the Bible six hundred and twenty four times while helper is mentioned only sixty-one times.

Man misunderstood the word servant to mean enslaving, to suppress and take away the rights of others. We misunderstood the word to mean claiming superiority over others and believing one ethnicity, or race, is better than the other.

A helper is more or less a mere worker without any commitment. The English dictionary describes a worker as “a labourer, a toiler, a hard helper, a slog or a hustler.” The same dictionary also describes a servant as “a person in the service of another”. Many of us often forget the fact that we are in the service of another person not in our own service.

'The word help in Hebrew is **azar** or **ezer**. It means “to protect, aid, help, succour, support, give material or nonmaterial encouragement.”

The Webster dictionary also describes **help** as "to aid, to assist, to succour, to lend strength or means towards affecting a purpose. To relieve, to cure, or to mitigate pain or disease. To remedy; to change for the better."

God did not need a helper, otherwise He would have created man first, to help Him in His work of creation. God is looking for a servant; someone who He can send to reach the lost, the hopeless, the Godless and the sick. Someone He can pour Himself into and reach the world.

God does not need helpers, otherwise He would have created man before heaven and earth. He did not employ any staff, neither did He use labourers to help Him create the universe.

Genesis. 1:1

In the beginning God created the heavens and the earth.

There is no denying the fact that it would require thousands upon thousands of helpers with different skills and millions of years to create the universe. Instead, God went about creating other things, including the animals, before He created mankind. In His omniscience, He is more than capable to do whatever He wants to do. All He is looking for are true servants, who want to serve Him in Spirit and in truth.

The office to which serving in the house of God refers to; is the Ministry of Helps. How I wish it was called the "Servants Ministry" because many of us took the word "Help" literarily.

The main purpose of our creation is to serve God. That was why God warned Pharaoh to let His people go, not for anything else but that they may serve Him. Pharaoh's refusal to do as God had commanded resulted in dire and untold consequences.

Exodus 8:1

And the Lord spake unto Moses, Go unto Pharaoh, and say unto him, Thus saith the Lord, Let my people go, that they may serve me.

We are not called to help, we are called to serve. When you help, you do what you like. You are in control of your time. You come in and you leave at your own convenience. The person you are helping waits on you, rather than you waiting on the person.

We are the ones who need help, not God. That is why after creating man, He looked at the man and said it is not good for a man to be alone. He proceeded to make man a helper. ***The Lord God said, "It is not good for the man to be alone. I will make a helper suitable for him." Genesis 2:18 (NIV).*** We not only need the physical help from our fellow man but also spiritual or divine help from God, who is the best help man can have.

No one is an island, whoever you may be; either an executive in a bank, the President of a nation, a Pastor in a church, or a labourer on a building sight, you are in the service of another person serving either vertically, horizontally, or laterally. It is therefore important that we understand who we are and the differences between a servant and a helper.

The problem we have in a majority of the so called third world countries, is that their leaders do not see themselves as servants of the people, otherwise they would have used their offices as leaders to serve the people better. Rather than serve the people, they serve and enrich themselves in the process. This explains why they embezzle the public funds and destroy millions of lives.

No wonder those who serve in government offices are referred to as 'civil' or 'public servants' (servants of the people) because they are answerable to the people. Many of our leaders see themselves as helpers as opposed to servants, answerable only to themselves. President Abraham Lincoln, the former US president defined democracy as: "Government of the people, by the people, for the people". Today, it has been turned around to mean "The government of me, by me, for me".

John 13:12

When he had finished washing their feet, he put on his clothes and returned to his place. "Do you understand what I have done for you?" he asked them.

Jesus is the supreme argument for a servant. He came purposely to serve mankind. All that He did was for mankind, not for Himself. He lived by an example that we should all emulate. He washed the feet of His disciples. Why should He wash their feet? After all He was supposed to be their "boss". He did not see himself as superior to His disciples neither did He consider washing their feet as a lowly, embarrassing and diminishing task. Christ came purposely to serve others.

Matthew 20:28

Just as the Son of Man did not come to be served, but to serve, and to give his life as a ransom for many."

God called us to serve Him with all our heart and everything that resides within us. We read of three kinds of servants in the Bible:

⇒ Those who are called and refuse instantly

⇒ Those that are called and answer immediately

⇒ Those that are called but answer later

THOSE WHO ARE CALLED AND REFUSE HIS CALLING.

A ruler asked Jesus in Matthew 19:16-22, what he has to do to have eternal life. Jesus told the man to keep the commandments. The man replied he already does and Jesus told him to go sell his belongings and follow Him. The man became dejected and went away sorrowfully.

Matthew 19:16-22

And, behold, one came and said unto him, Good Master, what good thing shall I do, that I may have eternal life?. And he said unto him, Why callest thou me good? there is none good but

one, that is, God: but if thou wilt enter into life, keep the commandments. He saith unto him, which? Jesus said, Thou shalt do no murder, Thou shalt not commit adultery, Thou shalt not steal, Thou shalt not bear false witness, Honour thy father and thy mother: and, Thou shalt love thy neighbour as thyself. The young man saith unto him, All these things have I kept from my youth up: what lack I yet? Jesus said unto him, If thou wilt be perfect, go and sell that thou hast, and give to the poor, and thou shalt have treasure in heaven: and come and follow me. But when the young man heard that saying, he went away sorrowful: for he had great possessions.

THOSE THAT ARE CALLED AND ANSWERED IMMEDIATELY

According to Matthew 4:18-22, Jesus called Peter and Andrew and they immediately followed Him. Again in verse 21, He called the sons of Zebedee, James and John, and they followed Him immediately.

Matthew 4:18-22

And Jesus, walking by the sea of Galilee, saw two brethren, Simon called Peter, and Andrew his brother, casting a net into the sea: for they were fishers. And he saith unto them, Follow me, and I will make you fishers of men. And they straightway left their nets, and followed him. And going on from thence, he saw other two brethren, James the son of Zebedee, and John his brother, in a ship with Zebedee their father, mending their nets; and he called them. And they immediately left the ship and their father, and followed him.

Those who are called but answer later

In 1 Kings Chapter 19, we read how Elijah cast his mantle upon Elisha. The Bible makes us understand that Elisha ran after Elijah and asked that he be allowed to go and kiss his parents goodbye before following the Prophet. Elijah bid him to go. Elisha went back and killed his oxen.

In killing the yoke of oxen, Elisha was making a strong commitment to follow and serve Elisha. He knew without his yoke of oxen, he could not return to his trade, or business, or his life as a farmer. He made sure of his total commitment to serve. He was so excited about his new calling and celebrated it with the people.

1 Kings 19:21 (NKJV)

So Elisha turned back from him, and took a yoke of oxen and slaughtered them and boiled their flesh, using the oxen's equipment, and gave it to the people, and they ate. Then he arose and followed Elijah, and became his servant.

You cannot be a servant of the Lord without being a servant of the people. You cannot see God or serve Him in person, but you can see his sons and daughters; for example, your brothers and sisters in the church, the sick, the poor, the strong, the weak and the needy. It is in the process of serving such people that you serve the Lord and others will serve you.

Every day of our lives, we are constantly faced with opportunities to serve someone. It could be at work, at home, in our communities or out on the street, but we often times focus more on our own interests. We have managed to build more or else a selfish and individualistic society.

As Christians we are not immune to serving. There have been so many shifts in recent years. We are becoming a self-conscious and self-centred group of people, not emulating our Master, Jesus Christ. Many of the charities we have today are the offshoot of Christian organisations of men and women who went to countries outside of their comfort zones to serve people. Christians such as Mary Slessor left Scotland to go to the remote village in Calabar, Nigeria as a missionary at a tender age of 28. Such people risk their lives in order to serve people.

These kind of missionaries write their goals and vision around the people they are supposed to serve, not around their personal needs and aspirations. They are givers not takers,' they listen not command, they carry out instructions not bury instructions, they obey not disobey, they function not dysfunction. They remain faithful to their subjects or masters, they are tolerant not intolerant. They are compassionate not selfish, they are careful not carefree.

Servants are observant and have their antenna constantly switched on.

Philippians 2:3-4

"Do nothing out of selfish ambition or vain conceit, but in humility consider others better than yourselves. Each of you should look not only to your own interests, but also to the interests of others".

Often times I tell stewards who serve under me that whatever they do in serving the Lord, they are doing it to themselves. Why? Because God does not need a new car, or a roof over His head.

Neither does He need clothes on His back, or food on His table. He already owns everything. ***For every beast of the forest is Mine, and the cattle on a thousand hills. (Psalm 50:10).***

He owns the cattle on a thousand hills. We are the ones looking forward to His blessings; we are the ones who need promotion and financial breakthrough. We are the ones who need divine favour or solutions to pressing issues. So technically speaking, whatever we do when we serve God, we do unto God but also for our own benefits.

Just one helper in your organisation, your group or in your team is one too many. They can be contagious and have the ability to multiply themselves. They are also divisive; they make people lose focus and affect the destiny of the people they make contact with. Let us examine the scripture below:

Acts15:36-41

Then after some days Paul said to Barnabas, "Let us now go back and visit our brethren in every city where we have preached the word of the Lord, and see how they are doing." Now Barnabas was determined to take with them John called Mark. But Paul insisted that they should not take with them the one who had departed from them in Pamphylia, and had not gone with them to the serve. Then the contention became so sharp that they parted from one another. And so Barnabas took Mark and sailed to Cyprus; but Paul chose Silas and departed, being commended by the brethren to the grace of God. And he went through Syria and Cilicia, strengthening the churches.

Paul and his team mate Barnabas, had both served the Lord and each other tirelessly. They found themselves disagreeing because of a "helper". Paul knew taking Mark with them to their next assignment would almost certainly derail their mission. He knew he could be a distraction citing his departure from them while they were in Pamphylia.

Barnabas was said to be determined to take Mark, which inevitably led to Paul and Barnabas parting ways. Paul, we learnt took Silas, while Barnabas took Mark. What happened indeed was that Paul took a "**servant**" while Barnabas took a "helper". The last three verses make it even more interesting: Paul and Silas went on from one city to another strengthening the churches while we never hear of Barnabas and Mark again.

⇒ True servanthood is **not about position, but production**. How productive are you? What is the quality of your service? Do you carry out the smallest task given to you with all diligence? What is your response to unfashionable tasks?

⇒ **True servanthood is not about your qualification, education, age or your years of service, but what makes the difference is the empowerment you give to others.** Whom have you empowered in your team lately? Do you always monopolise your knowledge in order to keep others out? Have you always watched your teammates struggle or waited for them to make detrimental mistakes?

TRUE SERVANTHOOD:

⇒ **Is about credibility.** We gain credibility when our service matches our actions and both in turn add value to other people. Proverb 17:2.

⇒ **It is about consistency.** How consistent are you? Do you give excuses when you don't feel like doing something? Do you only show up when it is convenient for you? Do you want it easy and without commitment?

⇒ **It is about going the extra mile.** What do you do when you are asked to go the extra mile?

⇒ **It is about the decision you make or take.** Do you make decisions based on how they benefit you or others?

⇒ **It is about your character.** Do you serve harder for your own image, in self aggrandisation, or do you serve harder for the team?

⇒ **It is about how faithful you are.** Are you faithful in handling the smaller responsibilities? ***Matthew 25:14-30.***

⇒ **It is about the anointing**

⇒ **It's about how diligent you are *"Not lagging in diligence, fervent in spirit, serving the Lord" Romans 12:10-11***

⇒ **It's about how humble you are. *"Serving the Lord in all humility with many tears and trials." Acts 20:19***

⇒ **It is about putting God first in everything.**

We must be content in any position we find ourselves no matter how small. There is more dignity in serving than there is in leading. If your actions and your thoughts towards your calling are wrong, then you are a helper and not a servant.

We all need help at one time or the other. It is great to have somebody to help you in your journey of life. However, the word 'Helpers' in the context of this book, is used to refer to stewards or workers who have chosen not to diligently serve God with their God given gifts and talents.

In the coming chapters, we will look more deeply into fifty-five differences between a helper and a servant.

#1

Helpers serve for momentary and measured gains, while Servants serve for endless and unmeasured rewards

Luke 16:13 (NIV)

"No one can serve two masters. Either you will hate the one and love the other, or you will be devoted to the one and despise the other. You cannot serve both God and money."

Matthew 6:19-21 (NIV)

"Do not store up for yourselves treasures on earth, where moths and vermin destroy, and where thieves break in and steal. But store up for yourselves treasures in heaven, where moths and vermin do not destroy, and where thieves do not break in and steal. For where your treasure is, there your heart will be also

Hebrews 13:5 (NIV)

Keep your lives free from the love of money and be content with what you have, because God has said, "Never will I leave you; never will I forsake you..

It is very common in this day and age to see "stewards" in churches being paid. As a matter of fact, some will insist that they

> ***They see their assignments or tasks only as a means to earn a living as opposed to serving the living God.***

will not serve unless they have the assurance of being paid. We live in an age where remuneration has taken over our commitment to serving God.

Please don't get me wrong, I am not implying that it is wrong to be remunerated in the house of the Lord, but not to the point where the Church of the Lord is being held to ransom.

I have heard of stewards in a church being paid each time they serve or as the case may be 'played'. They hold the whole church to ransom and care less about the people of God, because they see themselves as indispensable. I have also heard about stewards who go out to the secular world to "prostitute" their talents and don't see anything wrong with it all because of money.

I am not suggesting that people are to live in abject poverty or not benefit financially from their God given talents, after all their gifts are supposed to make room for them. What this book is saying is that success can't be to the detriment of serving God. We must not forget God gave this talent in the first place. You can liken this to a little boy who was given a bag of candies and a few minutes later was asked by the same person who gave him the candies to give one or two back but the boy refused.

Matthew 26:14-16

Then one of the twelve, called Judas Iscariot, went to the chief priests and said, "What are you willing to give me if I deliver Him to you?" And they counted out to him thirty pieces of silver. So from that time he sought opportunity to betray Him.

In this scripture, Judas set out to make money. He was ready to sell his master for momentary and measured gain. By so doing, he not only lost his life, he also missed out on witnessing the resurrection of Christ and the opportunity of receiving the Holy Ghost.

Helpers mortgage their God given talent for self-aggrandising ends. They came with the ultimate aim of earning as opposed to serving God. They see their assignments or tasks as a means to earn a living as opposed to serving the living God. They are only happy as long as the pay is right, reward is certain and promotion is assured. They are not committed beyond their pay, rewards, benefits or gains. They detach themselves from the goals, vision and aspiration of the organisation.

They are only happy as long as the pay is right, reward is certain and promotion is assured.

Just as Samson did, they merchandise their talent in the valley of Sorek, rather than to put it in use in the valley of Berakah (valley of praise). They regularly demand leadership role or positions and salary increase. They are never satisfied with what God is doing and don't know how to count their blessings.

Helpers want the title but not the responsibilities. They are highly motivated by money, self-enrichment and the pursuit of wealth.

A servant is the opposite. The goal and passion is always more important than the position and any financial reward.

#2

Helpers serve with the time in mind, while Servants serve to time

Luke 22:45-46

And when he rose up from prayer, and was come to his disciples, he found them sleeping for sorrow, and said unto them, Why sleep ye? Rise and pray, lest ye enter into temptation

Jesus had gone to Mount Olive with His disciples and called them to prayer. Upon His return, He met them sleeping. They couldn't wait because Jesus had gone for hours. How do we know this? Verse 44 says it all: ***And being in anguish, he prayed more earnestly, and his sweat was like drops of blood falling to the ground. Luke 22:44***

Kate serves in one of the most demanding departments in her local church. During the annual convention, serving stewards were asked to arrive at 9am. Kate arrives at an average time of about 10am every day, sighting delays in the train and buses. Kate spends a majority of the day taking time off for tea, or going for endless breaks. She shows up after tasks have been given out to other colleagues. Kate surely sees herself as a helper. She will only

They spend little or no time with the Bright and Morning Star but quantity and quality time with the movie stars.

serve on her own terms and not that of the department she serves in. She arrives at her own time and departs any time she desires. We have many people like Kate littered all over churches, serving in various departments today.

Absalom could not wait for his father David to die before assuming the throne. It was taking too long for him; he determined to turn the hands of the clock to achieve his purpose. When given an assignment or task, this kind of people keep a close eye on their watch, checking the time at regular intervals. They leave on the stroke of closing time, not caring if their task is completed or not. They arrive late, blaming the transport system as opposed to themselves. Their time is more important than that of the organisation. Staying behind or going the extra mile is a No! No! No!

They are highly likely to request that the organisation gives to them, rather than giving back to the organisation. They spend the organisations time surfing the internet or chatting on their mobile. Helpers complain if the service is too long, or the programs in the church are too many. They are very impatient and pay little attention to details. **They spend little or no time with the Bright and Morning Star but quantity and quality time with the movie stars.** They spend most of their time in front of the TV and have little or no time to read the Bible or pray.

#3

Helpers serve with rules, while Servants serve in rule

Matthew 9:9-13

As Jesus passed on from there, He saw a man named Matthew sitting at the tax office. And He said to him, "Follow Me." So he arose and followed Him. Now it happened, as Jesus sat at the table in the house that behold, many tax collectors and sinners came and sat down with Him and His disciples. And when the Pharisees saw it, they said to His disciples, "Why does your Teacher eat with tax collectors and sinners?" When Jesus heard that, He said to them, "Those who are well have no need of a physician, but those who are sick. But go and learn what this means: 'I desire mercy and not sacrifice.' For I did not come to call the righteous, but sinners, to repentance."

Mark 8:10

The Pharisees came and began to question Jesus. To test him, they asked him for a sign from heaven.

The Pharisees attached importance to Temple worship, but they had no personal relationship with God. They worship only for formal, religious observance, not because they seek to have a relationship with God or worship Him for who He is.

Helpers major on the don'ts and minor on the do's. They master on the negatives and are blind to the positives.

They were the custodians of the Mosaic Law. In an attempt to be seen as the ultimate authority, they added to the law, which was handed to Moses on Mount Sinai. They took this guideline to such extremes that the original written law was made of no effect by their oral laws and traditions.

Throughout the three and half years of Jesus' ministry the Pharisees and the Sadducees constantly threw the "rule book" at Jesus every time He tried to do what He was sent to do by His father. They set traps to catch Him on many occasions. How often do you come across stewards like this, who are quick to throw the "rule book" at you?

Helpers major on the don'ts and minor on the do's. They are masters of the negatives and are blind to the positives. They are holier than holy and have a religious spirit, always misquoting the scripture out of context. Outwardly they live blameless lives, but inwardly their attitudes are abominable. They know all the laws and commandments and watch over them. They carry the biggest Bible around but don't meditate in it day and night. Their Bible is for mere decoration.

They are hypocritical and very judgmental; quick to judge others but cover up their own sins. They seek to remove the plank from others people's eyes and ignore the plank in their own eyes. They are spiritually blind. They question their leader's good intentions and turn it around to mean evil. They believe they are experts in everything and always have an opinion on every issue. They must always have the last say.

#4

Helpers work-to-rule, while Servants serve in full

Proverb 22:13

The slothful man saith, there is a lion without; I shall be slain in the streets.

The dictionary definition of work-to-rule is: "Where employees do no more than the minimum required by the rules of a workplace in order to cause a slowdown." A work-to-rule man will give flimsy excuses. He is slothful and can be very laid back. He is so indifferent to everything within the organisation or department he belongs to.

They are difficult to motivate. They benefit from whatever motivating methods you employ but it takes them little or no time to revert to their usual pattern. **Helpers are unteachable, untouchable, unreasonable and unbearable.** They are rigid and inflexible.

On the contrary, servants are diligent in all they do. They see tasks through, never content with one task. They are constantly looking for something else to do.

1 Corinthians 15:58

But by the grace of God I am what I am: and his grace which was bestowed upon me was not in vain; but I laboured more abundantly than they all: yet not I, but the grace of God which was with me.

Proverbs 22:29

Seest thou a man diligent in his business? He shall stand before kings; he shall not stand before mean men.

Abraham was such a blessed man, he was said to be very rich in cattle and was surrounded by many servants. His son Isaac was so laid back; to the point that he couldn't find a wife for himself. He was 40 years old when a woman was betrothed to him. Abraham had to send out one of his trusted servants to go and find his son a wife. Abraham knew Isaac was comfortable with his position and status as the son of the richest man. He was such a spoilt brat that even when Rebecca was brought to him, the first thing he did was to take her to his mother's tent.

Genesis 24:1-4

And Abraham was old, and well stricken in age: and the Lord had blessed Abraham in all things. And Abraham said unto his eldest servant of his house, that ruled over all that he had, Put, I pray thee, thy hand under my thigh: And I will make thee swear by the Lord, the God of heaven, and the God of the earth, that thou shalt not take a wife unto my son of the daughters of the Canaanites, among whom I dwell: but thou shalt go unto my country, and to my kindred, and take a wife unto my son Isaac.

#5

Helpers serve in pride, while Servants serve with pride

Daniel 4:30-32

The king spake, and said, Is not this great Babylon, that I have built for the house of the kingdom by the might of my power, and for the honour of my majesty? While the word was in the king's mouth, there fell a voice from heaven, saying, O king Nebuchadnezzar, to thee it is spoken; The kingdom is departed from thee. And they shall drive thee from men, and thy dwelling shall be with the beasts of the field: they shall make thee to eat grass as oxen, and seven times shall pass over thee, until thou know that the most High ruleth in the kingdom of men, and giveth it to whomsoever he will.

Daniel 5:20-21

But when his heart was lifted up, and his mind hardened in pride, he was deposed from his kingly throne, and they took his glory from him. And he was driven from the sons of men; and his heart was made like the beasts, and his dwelling was with the wild asses: they fed him with grass like oxen, and his body was wet with the dew of heaven; till he knew that the

most high God ruled in the kingdom of men, and that he appointeth over it whomsoever he will.

King Nebuchadnezzar, the King of Babylon was so arrogant and full of himself that it got him into trouble with God. He did not recognise that his achievement and greatness as King was because of the grace of God. He thought he was self-made.

How many times have you heard someone talk so much about their success that they leave God out of it? They forget the time when they prayed for the blessing of the womb and when the child came, they stop serving and start blaming the child. They are proud of their educational achievements and look down on their colleagues who may not be as educated as they are. Any leader placed over them with less education or privileged background is undermined and always subjected to torture and abuse. They are rude and arrogant; they disrespect others and are always full of themselves. They believe the manager or leader doesn't know how to do anything.

They are stubborn and more likely to set their own objectives. They believe they are better than the manager or leader and get angry if their suggestions are not adopted.

Nebuchadnezzar's pride got him into trouble and he ended up with the animals. Servants, on the other hand, are proud of their faith and their task.

#6

Helpers are sheep chasers, while Servants are sheep keepers

Luke 15:1-6

Now the tax collectors and sinners were all gathering around to hear Jesus. But the Pharisees and the teachers of the law muttered, "This man welcomes sinners and eats with them." Then Jesus told them this parable: "Suppose one of you has a hundred sheep and loses one of them. Doesn't he leave the ninety-nine in the open country and go after the lost sheep until he finds it? And when he finds it, he joyfully puts it on his shoulders and goes home. Then he calls his friends and neighbours together and says, 'Rejoice with me; I have found my lost sheep.

The story was told of an usher in a Pentecostal church in Nigeria. A young lady who lived in the United States of America for some years, during the days of Afro hair styles returned home and was invited to this church. After much persuasion, she reluctantly agreed to go.

This church believe women should cover their head when they are in church, but this young lady, who came from a different background and was unaware of the tradition wore her afro hair

> ***Sheep chasers are drill masters, with a sergeant major mentality. They see themselves as the custodian of the organisation's "ten commandments".***

style with much pride. One of the ushers spotted the young lady as she came in, and walked towards her. She immediately summoned the visitor out and brought out a scruffy dirty scarf. The usher asked the lady to wear it on her head as it is unacceptable for women to leave their heads uncovered in that denomination. The young lady was so embarrassed and was made to feel unwelcome. The end result was that the lady never returned to the church. No one saw her again, that sure is a loss of a soul.

In my local church one Sunday morning, the praise was so powerful that you could feel the presence of the Holy Spirit. It was so powerful that many people were crying and rolling on the floor. There was no doubting God's presence. I was tapped on the shoulder by one of the ushers who was wearing what seemed a disturbed look. I quickly followed her to the reception to find out what the problem was. Immediately, I saw a middle age gentleman who seemed to be in distress. Sitting close to him were two altar workers. She explained to me that during the praise and worship, the man had been repeatedly shouting "let go of me I don't want to stay here". I asked the gentleman be brought out so we can minister to him.

This man told me he is from Africa and he felt very uncomfortable in the service. He said he was involved in all kinds of atrocities during the struggle for independence and against apartheid. I believed the fire of God was too much for him but he was reluctant to yield to the call of God to repentance. I tried to minister to the gentleman for 30 minutes or more. I tried to explain to him that God loves him irrespective of what he may have done and all he needs to do is to confess his sin and accept Christ as his personal saviour and his sins will be forgiven. After much persuasion, I eventually led him to Christ. I must say he still insisted he wanted to leave but at least he gave his life. I am sure heaven was rejoicing for another addition to God's kingdom. We planted the seed and God, I believe has not stopped watering the seed, who knows if this guy is on fire for God somewhere now.

Jesus gave the parable of the lost sheep in Luke 15:3-6. Notice what the Pharisees where murmuring about. That Jesus welcomed sinners. They saw themselves as being more righteous than the people. They saw themselves holy and sinless. We have folks in church who sometimes behave likewise.

Helpers always think they are more important and better than others. They label anyone who looks, dresses or speaks differently to them. They form a group with other people of like minds and alienate others. They scatter the sheep with their actions and their mouths. They are not sensitive to other people's needs or concerns. Sheep chasers are drill masters, with a sergeant major mentality. They see themselves as the custodian of the organisation's “ten commandments". They are regimental in their approach. Their “don'ts” far exceeds their “do's. “They are quick to throw the stones but slow to administer love and forgiveness.

True servants are welcoming and accommodating. They are excited for every new addition to the church. They celebrate others and accept them for who they are.

#7

Helpers serve according to their own purpose, while Servants serve according to God's purpose

Judges 13:3-5

The angel of the Lord appeared to her and said, "You are barren and childless, but you are going to become pregnant and give birth to a son. Now see to it that you drink no wine or other fermented drink and that you do not eat anything unclean. You will become pregnant and have a son whose head is never to be touched by a razor because the boy is to be a Nazirite, dedicated to God from the womb. He will take the lead in delivering Israel from the hands of the Philistines."

Judges 14:1-4

Samson went down to Timnah and saw there a young Philistine woman. When he returned, he said to his father and mother, "I have seen a Philistine woman in Timnah; now get her for me as my wife." His father and mother replied, "Isn't there an acceptable woman among your relatives or among all our people? Must you go to the uncircumcised Philistines to get a wife? " But Samson said to his father, "Get her for me. She's the right one for me." (His parents did not know that

this was from the Lord, who was seeking an occasion to confront the Philistines; for at that time they were ruling over Israel.)

Luke 15:11-32

And he said, a certain man had two sons: And the younger of them said to his father, Father, give me the portion of goods that falleth to me. And he divided unto them his living. And not many days after the younger son gathered all together, and took his journey into a far country, and there wasted his substance with riotous living.

Samson was set aside by God even before he was born. He was chosen to deliver Israel from the hands of the Philistines. However, Samson became selfish and went about fulfilling his own purpose. He was supposed to live the life of a Nazarene but failed to live up to expectation. He was endowed with incredible strength, ability and understanding. Every step he took was inadvertently designed to further his own selfish ends. He was set aside by God for a purpose and preserved even through difficult times. However, he failed to live a purposeful life. His lifestyle was nothing to write home about. Such people are selfish and never able to embrace change. They are likely to revolt if any change is going to affect their daily routine. They are repetitive and lack vision. They are like a frog in the kettle on a gas fire. The frog keeps adjusting itself until it's cooked.

This group of people sometimes misplace the purpose of their calling and are quick to form ungodly relationships. Anything they do is motivated by a personal inclination of revenge, rather than a desire to establish the purpose of God. They misuse their ability

> ***They are like a frog in the kettle on a gas fire. The frog keeps adjusting itself until it's cooked.***

and strength by focusing on things that are ungodly. They allow their desires (weaknesses) to cloud their sense of judgment. They focus so much on themselves and allow anger to take root in their heart. They have little or no compassion and never utilise the blessings and grace of God at their disposal. They constantly fail to understand the grace and the anointing of God upon their lives and they do not comprehend the power that resides in the purpose of God for them.

Many of us must have come across people who have lived wasted lives. We see young men and women who walk the streets of major cities in the world. Along the line, they may have ignored the wisdom of their parents, teachers or mentor and chosen to follow their devil-given purpose.

#8

Helpers serve with promotion in mind, while Servants serve with promotion assured

Genesis 12:1-3 (NKJV)

Now the Lord had said to Abram: "Get out of your country, from your family and from your father's house, to a land that I will show you. I will make you a great nation; I will bless you and make your name great; and you shall be a blessing. I will bless those who bless you, and I will curse him who curses you; and in you all the families of the earth shall be blessed."

Mark 10:34-40 (NIV)

Then James and John, the sons of Zebedee, came to him. "Teacher," they said, "we want you to do for us whatever we ask." "What do you want me to do for you?" he asked. They replied, "Let one of us sit at your right and the other at your left in your glory." "You don't know what you are asking," Jesus said. "Can you drink the cup I drink or be baptized with the baptism I am baptized with?" "We can," they answered. Jesus said to them, "You will drink the cup I drink and be baptized with the baptism I am baptized with but to sit at my right or left is not for me to grant. These places belong to

those for whom they have been prepared." When the ten heard about this, they became indignant with James and John. Jesus called them together and said, "You know that those who are regarded as rulers of the Gentiles lord it over them, and their high officials exercise authority over them. Not so with you. Instead, whoever wants to become great among you must be your servant and whoever wants to be first must be slave of all. For even the Son of Man did not come to be served, but to serve, and to give his life as a ransom for many."

How desperate can people be? In their quest for power and promotion, James and John recruited their mother to seek for position in the Kingdom of God. What a bizarre situation. They went to great lengths to seek for power, by reason of their relationship with Jesus. I wouldn't say these two disciples came to Jesus because of power but I would not be wrong to say that at some point in their walk with Christ, they felt they could do with some kind of recognition. They wanted a promotion at all costs.

This kind of desperation creates division among others, or within the department. It brings the department or organisation into disrepute, and compromises the authority and the power of the leaders. It brings unhealthy rivalry among team members and can seriously affect the morale of team members. These people are aggressive and disrespectful and can't see anything good in others. They can be very abusive, defensive and argumentative and like to cut corners. They are always angry and jealous of their colleagues. They can also be manipulative, destructive and power drunk. They sow seeds of discord with the aim of finding or recruiting allies. They fail to realise position is greater when it is earned, bestowed or by divine appointment. Such people are selective with what they want to believe and can use their gifts to win people over. They are over ambitious and cowardly, weak and pretentious. They have an appetite for good things but are impatient to wait, or serve for it. These people lack what it takes to control their appetite. They join the department or company with one thing in mind; how to be in control, how to be the leader.

Many of us want position but we are not ready to sacrifice our time, energy and our money. We fail to realise that as responsibility increases, rights decrease. Servants understand the importance of developing the spirit of long-suffering. They are ready to serve others first and serve their way up. They are steadfast, never wavering or compromise. As servants, our position or title must have less to do with our ego but more to do with the people we are called to influence, touch or serve. It is important that we understand that we can make a difference in whatever task or role we are given.

1 Kings 1:5

Then Adonijah the son of Haggith exalted himself, saying, "I will be king"; and he prepared for himself chariots and horsemen, and fifty men to run before him.

Let us also examine the story of Adonijah, King David's son. It is an oxymoron, the fact that Adonijah was alive and saw his brother Absalom try to take away his father's throne and end up losing his life, even though he was supported by some of King David's henchmen or lieutenants. You would have thought any sensible man would learn from Absalom's over ambition, but Adonijah didn't.

It could be argued that Adonijah was the heir to the throne and his attempt to snatch the throne away from his father David was justifiable. Adonijah was the fourth born son of David and was born after Absalom. Now that Absalom was dead, he was the next in line. Besides, his father did not make it easy for him by remaining silent and not making any public announcement or endorsement of any of his other sons. Adonijah became over ambitious and allowed this to cloud his reasoning and his level of judgment. All the while, there was one thing he had in mind: how to be the King. His overwhelming desire for instant power distorted his ability to learn from his brother‘s deadly mistakes.

#9

Helpers stand up to their masters, while Servants stands up for their masters

Numbers 12:1-10

And Miriam and Aaron spake against Moses because of the Ethiopian woman whom he had married: for he had married an Ethiopian woman. And they said, Hath the Lord indeed spoken only by Moses? hath he not spoken also by us? And the Lord heard it. Now the man Moses was very meek, above all the men which were upon the face of the earth. And the Lord spake suddenly unto Moses, and unto Aaron, and unto Miriam, Come out ye three unto the tabernacle of the congregation. And they three came out. And the Lord came down in the pillar of the cloud, and stood in the door of the tabernacle, and called Aaron and Miriam: and they both came forth. And he said, hear now my words: If there be a prophet among you, I the Lord will make myself known unto him in a vision, and will speak unto him in a dream. My servant Moses is not so, who is faithful in all mine house. With him will I speak mouth to mouth, even apparently, and not in dark speeches; and the similitude of the Lord shall he behold: wherefore then were ye not afraid to speak against my

servant Moses? And the anger of the Lord was kindled against them; and he departed. And the cloud departed from off the tabernacle; and, behold, Miriam became leprous, white as snow: and Aaron looked upon Miriam, and, behold, she was leprous.

The scripture above recorded the rebellion of Miriam and Aaron against their brother Moses. They stood up to their brother and questioned his position and authority over Israel because of his marriage to an Ethiopian woman. The actions of this brother and sister in crime so angered the Lord that He called them to a meeting at the City Hall; the tabernacle of the congregation. There He made His disapproval of their conduct known.

To rebel against the authority of your leader is tantamount to rebellion against the authority of God.

Matthew made a strong and powerful statement about God's servants in ***Matthew 10:40: "He that receiveth you receiveth me, and he that receiveth me receiveth him that sent me"***. When you stand up to your leader or your Pastor, you are automatically pressing a self-destruct button.

Stewards like this are impatient. They will stop at nothing until they get what they want.

A young man who without any shadow of doubt had God's calling upon his life serves as a steward in one of the demanding departments in a local church. He was very dedicated and always there to serve whatever the situation. He applied himself diligently to the ministry God called him into. However, he became so carried away that he began to disagree with the leader, objecting to whatever he did or suggested. It was not long before he began to criticise him publicly and rebel against him telling other members of the team to disobey him.

Numbers 16:1-3

Korah son of Izhar, the son of Kohath, the son of Levi, and certain Reubenites—Dathan and Abiram, sons of Eliab, and On son of Peleth—became insolent and rose up against Moses. With them were 250 Israelite men, well-known community leaders who had been appointed members of the council. They came as a group to oppose Moses and Aaron and said to them, "You have gone too far! The whole community is holy, every one of them, and the Lord is with them. Why then do you set yourselves above the Lord's assembly?"

Korah, Kohath and Abiram also rose up against Moses and Aaron. Their end result was total destruction. The ground under them split apart and the earth opened its mouth and swallowed them and their household up.

Exodus 32:25-26

Moses saw that the people were running wild and that Aaron had let them get out of control and so become a laughingstock to their enemies. So he stood at the entrance to the camp and said, "Whoever is for the Lord, come to me." And all the Levites rallied to him.

A similar account was recorded in Exodus 32:25-26. The children of Israel exerted so much pressure on Aaron that they subsequently forced his hands to make a god for them to worship. The event occurred when Moses had gone to the mountain to meet with God. Upon his arrival, Moses was so enraged he destroyed the image.

Something more interesting then happened. Moses asked those who remained on the Lord's side, to come to him. The Levites were the only tribe that rallied to Moses. They stood up for their master by aligning themselves with him. They recognised that the position of Moses was of authority and power. They recognised and respected the anointing upon his life. Although they were part of the whole congregation that sinned, the Levites were quick to recognise their folly and turned from their wrongs. They stood by their master, rather than rebel against him.

To rebel against the authority of your leader is tantamount to rebellion against the authority of God.

#10

Helpers serve with "spikes-on," while Servants serve "in spite of"

Daniel 3:16-18

Shadrach, Meshach, and Abed–nego, answered and said to the king, O Nebuchadnezzar, we are not careful to answer thee in this matter. If it be so, our God whom we serve is able to deliver us from the burning fiery furnace, and he will deliver us out of thine hand, O king. But if not, be it known unto thee, O king that we will not serve thy gods, nor worship the golden image which thou hast set up.

The Encyclopaedia describes spikes as pointed protrusions, usually made of metal, ceramic or plastic that is screwed into the bottom of most track and field shoes to increase traction and minimise the likelihood of slipping. Many young women wear long pointed shoes today to make a fashion statement. Although attractive, and as much as it helps to enhance or augment the height of such women, you would not wish for them to step on your toes wearing such shoes. If they do, I can guarantee you would see stars and hear the rolling thunder. You will certainly feel untold excruciating pain to your very bone marrow. You are likely to sustain a wound that will take a long time to heal, or if the heel caught you in a bad place the discomfort may last a life time.

Such is the pain some church folks are subjected to by these people described above. They wear their "spikes" with pride twenty-four seven. They step on everyone as they go along not minding if they are hurting people or not. Every statement they make is poisonous and heart piercing.

They wear their "spikes" with pride twenty-four seven. They step on everyone as they go along not minding if they are hurting people or not. Every statement they make is poisonous and heart piercing.

Matthew 2:16

Then Herod, when he saw that he was deceived by the wise men, was exceedingly angry; and he sent forth and put to death all the male children who were in Bethlehem and in all its districts, from two years old and under, according to the time which he had determined from the wise men.

In the scripture above, King Herod set out to kill every male child in Bethlehem and its vicinity, who was two years old and under. His main aim was to kill Jesus. He was ready to destroy anyone that got in his way. People like this can destroy in seconds with their mouths not caring whether you are hurt or not. They pierce you in the ribs with the ultimate aim of demoralising you. They knock other colleagues and backbite. They undermine and cause strife among colleagues. They are unable to control their anger and forever complain about virtually everything.

A servant will never complain as long as what he or she is asked to do glorifies God. They are sold out and serve the Lord regardless of their pain or abuse. It does not matter whether they are rich or poor, or what people say about them.

#11

Helpers serve only when they are at base, while Servants serve from wherever they are based

Acts 8:26-40

And the angel of the Lord spake unto Philip, saying, Arise, and go toward the south unto the way that goeth down from Jerusalem unto Gaza, which is desert. And he arose and went: and, behold, a man of Ethiopia, an eunuch of great authority under Candace queen of the Ethiopians, who had the charge of all her treasure, and had come to Jerusalem for to worship,

In medical practice, doctors are sometimes required to be on call. To be on call means; being available and ready at short notice to come in and attend to patients. This is because they deal with life and death issues.

Phillip was minding his own business when the Angel of the Lord appeared to him to leave the comfort of his home in the city and go to the middle of a desert in Gaza. Phillip, we learn, arose and went. He did not complain to the Angel about being asked to do such a job at short notice, neither did he complain of being sent to a desert. He was ready to take on any task from wherever, be it at home, on the road at Church or anywhere.

If a new church is to be planted in New York and another one in a remote village in Africa where there is no light, no water, nor any other basic amenities, you can rest assured the planting church will not be short of Pastors who would want to go to New York. On the other hand, it would almost certainly be a struggle to fill the position in Africa.

As a servant you must be ready to be called at any time, even at what some may call unsociable hours, or to take on unfashionable duty. What would you do if you are being summoned by your Pastor at 2am in the morning to intercede for a member of the church whose life is in danger, or if you were asked to visit someone in the hospital? **Your expectation as a servant is not limited to what you do when you are in the church but also to what you do at home and in your leisure time.**

If you reconcile to only serve when you are in church, or at your own convenience, and you don't make yourself available outside the church hours, then you are a helper. I recall a steward who served in my local church some years back. She was only available to serve on Sundays but not Monday to Saturday. She would refuse to answer her phone if you call her any other day. Your service to the Lord, or to your local church should not be limited to only while you are in the church.

Helpers only serve with time. They are not committed beyond their desk or task. They won't go the extra mile. They embrace there comfort zone and pitch a tent around it. A servant however is the opposite, they serve anytime and they are ready to stand up, line up and battle on. A true servant puts God first in everything.

#12

Helpers play around with their assignments, while Servants stay on top of their assignments

1 Samuel 15:1-10

Samuel also said unto Saul, The Lord sent me to anoint thee to be king over his people, over Israel: now therefore hearken thou unto the voice of the words of the Lord. Thus saith the Lord of hosts, I remember that which Amalek did to Israel, how he laid wait for him in the way, when he came up from Egypt. Now go and smite Amalek, and utterly destroy all that they have, and spare them not; but slay man and woman, infant and suckling, ox and sheep, camel and ass. And Saul gathered the people together, and numbered them in Telaim, two hundred thousand footmen, and ten thousand men of Judah. And Saul came to a city of Amalek, and laid wait in the valley. And Saul said unto the Kenites, Go, depart, get you down from among the Amalekites, lest I destroy you with them: for ye shewed kindness to all the children of Israel, when they came up out of Egypt. So the Kenites departed from among the Amalekites. And Saul smote the Amalekites from Havilah until thou comest to Shur, that is over against Egypt. And he took Agag the king of the Amalekites alive, and utterly

destroyed all the people with the edge of the sword. But Saul and the people spared Agag, and the best of the sheep, and of the oxen, and of the fatlings, and the lambs, and all that was good, and would not utterly destroy them: but everything that was vile and refuse, that they destroyed utterly.

Moses' main assignment on earth was to deliver the children of Israel from slavery. Because of his inability to stay focused, he spent the first 80 years of his life playing around. It was after this age that he started fulfilling the purpose of his creation. Moses did not take his assignment seriously. He focused his attention on other assignments.

Stewards like this are never at their desk or hands on with the tasks they are given. They lack concentration and are always late. They give excuse after excuse, take endless breaks and a long time off. They play around and never take the things of God, their salvation and their spiritual life seriously. They focus more on the mundane things of life, things that are not relevant. They are more conscious of their appearance; the clothes they wear on Sunday to church and their hair style. They come to church and want to be like the Joneses; they run into unnecessary debt because they want to drive a better car than Mr & Mrs Jones.

Servants on the other hand make their spiritual development a priority and they are still able to look good, smell good and drive the car of their choice.

#13

Helpers serve with many masters, while Servants serve with one master

Matthew 6:24

No man can serve two masters: for either he will hate the one, and love the other; or else he will hold to the one, and despise the other. Ye cannot serve God and mammon.

2 Corinthians 6:14

Do not be unequally yoked with unbelievers. For what partnership has righteousness with lawlessness? Or what fellowship has light with darkness

Exodus 20:1-7

And God spake all these words, saying, I am the Lord thy God, which have brought thee out of the land of Egypt, out of the house of bondage. Thou shalt have no other gods before me.

God gave an affirmative word to Moses for the children of Israel; that they should not serve any other god apart from Him. However, we see so many kings not following in the footsteps of David their father. They tried to serve God and in most cases created an image to worship. The Bible recorded accounts of some of the kings who did not walk in the ways of their father.

King Ahab and his wife Jezebel decided the God of their fathers and Israel was not enough. They decided to serve and worship Baal. Ahab set up an altar for Baal in the temple. God had to send Elijah to destroy all the prophets of Baal on the same mount He gave Moses the Commandments.

They have breakfast at St Peters, lunch at the communion Pentecostal Church and dinner at The Church of Christ The Immaculate.

1 Kings 18:20-21

So Ahab sent unto all the children of Israel, and gathered the prophets together unto mount Carmel. And Elijah came unto all the people, and said, How long halt ye between two opinions? if the Lord be God, follow him: but if Baal, then follow him. And the people answered him not a word.

When you serve two masters you have divided love and divided loyalty. You are neither here nor there. You become a double minded person and you become unstable. You are never satisfied with what you have. This kind of person jumps from one ministry to another, claiming God told them to move. Their heart is always somewhere else, seeking for what they already have. They are never satisfied with their Pastor. They nurture the notion "the grass is greener on the other side of town". **They have breakfast at St Peters, lunch at the Communion Pentecostal Church and dinner at The Church of Christ The Immaculate.**

#14

Helpers sell their birth right, while Servants guard over their birth right

Genesis 25:29-34

And Jacob sod pottage: and Esau came from the field, and he was faint: And Esau said to Jacob, Feed me, I pray thee, with that same red pottage; for I am faint: therefore was his name called Edom. And Jacob said, Sell me this day thy birthright. And Esau said, Behold, I am at the point to die: and what profit shall this birthright do to me? And Jacob said, Swear to me this day; and he sware unto him: and he sold his birthright unto Jacob. Then Jacob gave Esau bread and pottage of lentiles; and he did eat and drink, and rose up, and went his way: thus Esau despised his birthright.

Esau couldn't control himself and for one moment of madness, he gave away his birth right for a pot of porridge. The brother of the prodigal son kept his right, he knew the importance of waiting, he knew his inheritance was assured; even if it hadn't manifested yet.

It is now increasingly common for associate Ministers to become impatient because they believe God has called them to be a Pastor or an Evangelist. They launch themselves immediately, demanding the right to leave and start their own ministry. They do not realise that receiving the revelation of being a Pastor does not necessarily mean it must happen straightaway. There has to be a period of waiting, training, moulding and shaping.

Imagine Elisha asking Elijah to release him because he believed he had the calling of God upon his life. He would never have received the mantle and would have missed the double portion of Elijah's anointing. He would have ended up being an ordinary prophet. Over the years I have seen many people sell their birth rights by bailing out of a "fighter jet" without any parachute. They end up crash landing. Elisha was determined to keep his birth right. Even at the point where he was to receive the mantle from Elijah, a handful of his mates tried to talk to him out of his birth right.

Luke 15:28-32

And he was angry, and would not go in: therefore came his father out, and intreated him. And he answering said to his father, Lo, these many years do I serve thee, neither transgressed I at any time thy commandment: and yet thou never gavest me a kid, that I might make merry with my friends: But as soon as this thy son was come, which hath devoured thy living with harlots, thou hast killed for him the fatted calf. And he said unto him, Son, thou art ever with me, and all that I have is thine. It was meet that we should make merry, and be glad: for this thy brother was dead, and is alive again; and was lost, and is found.

In the scripture above, the prodigal son's brother grew angry and protested against his father's bizarre celebration of his brother, who had claimed his inheritance and squandered it. But notice what his father said in verse 31' he said to him; "you are always with me and everything I have is yours". In other words, he is saying, “come on son, you have kept your birth right while your brother lost his. You have kept and preserved your inheritance, you have been patient, your future is assured my son, you have been faithful and loyal, and you stand to inherit everything I have.”

#15

Helpers serve in vain, while Servants serve to avail

Isaiah 65:23

They shall not labour in vain, nor bring forth for trouble; for they are the seed of the blessed of the LORD, and their offspring with them. And it shall come to pass, that before they call, I will answer; and while they are yet speaking, I will hear. (God will not forget your labour of love).

1 Corinthians 15:58

But by the grace of God I am what I am: and his grace which was bestowed upon me was not in vain; but I laboured more abundantly than they all: yet not I, but the grace of God which was with me.

The English dictionary describes vain as: being proud of one's appearance, possessions or achievement; worthless, senseless or futile; not giving due respect to whom respect is due. On the other hand, the same dictionary describes avail as; to make a difference, a mark of respect or meekness, to be of use, to be in a position of advantage, to profit, to make use of, to be privileged.

You cannot serve God with self-righteousness or hold yourself to such high regard far beyond others. It wouldn't be long before you begin to arrogate yourself, claiming rights to everything that is done in your department. It wouldn't be long before you start to disrespect your colleagues and your leaders. You would become so possessive, claiming the successes within the department as your own. Such an attitude creates a tense atmosphere within a team. These people are so bossy and controlling, seeking control over every task and the team including its leader.

When your main objective is to make a difference within a team, not minding whether you are acknowledged for what you did or not; when you are happy for others to be at the forefront and you take the back seat, making an impact and making a difference, your labour of love will not be forgotten. The fruit of your labour will be evident for people to see.

#16

Helpers serve and faint, while Servants serve and renew their strength

Isaiah 40:31

But they that wait upon the LORD shall renew their strength; they shall mount up with wings as eagles; they shall run, and not be weary; and they shall walk, and not faint.

There are a number of biblical examples of people who waited upon the Lord and were able to achieve their objectives:

⇒ Abraham and Sarah while they waited for Isaac

⇒ Joseph while he was in prison

⇒ Christ Jesus while he waited for His time to be fulfilled

⇒ Mary and Martha; while they waited for Jesus to arrive when Lazarus their brother was lying dead. John 11:1-43

⇒ The ruler of the synagogue; Jarius' father. He stayed with Jesus and waited on Him while He attended to another sick woman; despite his daughter being at the point of death

Equally, there were also people who couldn't wait and fainted along the way.

⇒ The prodigal son. He couldn't wait for his father to die before he took over his possession.

⇒ Absalom son of King David. He became so desperate for his father's throne.

Luke 15:11-32(NKJV)

Then He said: "A certain man had two sons. And the younger of them said to his father, 'Father, give me the portion of goods that falls to me.' So he divided to them his livelihood. And not many days after, the younger son gathered all together, journeyed to a far country, and there wasted his possessions with prodigal living. But when he had spent all, there arose a severe famine in that land, and he began to be in want. Then he went and joined himself to a citizen of that country, and he sent him into his fields to feed swine. And he would gladly have filled his stomach with the pods that the swine ate, and no one gave him anything. "But when he came to himself, he said, 'How many of my father's hired servants have bread enough and to spare, and I perish with hunger! I will arise and go to my father, and will say to him, "Father, I have sinned against heaven and before you, and I am no longer worthy to be called your son. Make me like one of your hired servants."'

As you wait on Him, you rely upon His strength, His love and His promise. It is about relying on Him, committing our all to Him. Not bowing to our own self will; not giving up or throwing in the towel. You are guaranteed an effortless service.

#16

The prodigal son was in haste to inherit his father's fortune. While he was still at home, all that his father owned belong to him and his brother but he was not ready to wait. He went to a far country with the money given to him by his father and wasted everything. He spent and spent until he ended up eating the leftovers meant for pigs. He gave in to his own will and believed in his ability to sustain and manage his new found wealth. He became selfish and wasteful. He lost his good sense of rationale and morality. He forgot his dignity and whose son he was; the result was a broken and fainted man; a man who couldn't swim in the very deep end of a river; he was gasping for breath.

#17

Helpers soil the hands of their master, while Servants wash the hands of their master

2 Kings 3:11

But Jehoshaphat said, is there not here a prophet of the Lord, that we may enquire of the Lord by him? And one of the king of Israel's servants answered and said, Here is Elisha the son of Shaphat, which poured water on the hands of Elijah.

Jonah 1:1-4

Now the word of the Lord came unto Jonah the son of Amittai, saying, Arise, go to Nineveh, that great city, and cry against it; for their wickedness is come up before me. But Jonah rose up to flee unto Tarshish from the presence of the Lord, and went down to Joppa; and he found a ship going to Tarshish: so he paid the fare thereof, and went down into it, to go with them unto Tarshish from the presence of the Lord. But the Lord sent out a great wind into the sea, and there was a mighty tempest in the sea, so that the ship was like to be broken.

Elisha spent ten years just washing the hands of Elijah ***(2 Kings Chapter 3:11)***. He was also described as; ***"He who poured water on the hands of Elijah."*** Each time, after Elijah had finished eating,

Elisha would bring some water and pour it out for Elijah to wash his hands. He did that job so regularly and faithfully that he was described by it. God will test our faithfulness in little things before He commits a ministry to us. Joshua served Moses faithfully for many years before he became the next leader. Timothy served Paul faithfully and became an Apostle.

Sometimes you may have to carry out unfashionable tasks without feeling embarrassed or belittled. I am not sure how many of us would be happy if asked to do unfashionable tasks everyday such as cleaning the toilet. Washing the hands of a man can be seen to be unglamorous and unfashionable. Doing such tasks daily can compound and magnify it in this modern day, and would probably be seen as an abuse of power and authority.

What is it that you consider unfashionable, what would you not do for God? In the book of ***Jonah 1:1-4***, Jonah was asked by God to go to Nineveh to preach repentance, but instead, he went to Tarshish. He felt the job was not for him and God would need to find another person to do His "dirty work". He felt he would rather keep his hands clean and couldn't care less if Jesus' hands were soiled or dirty. He would have preferred a more glamorous city, where God had been universally accepted and everyone was saved. He would have preferred to preach about a much more receptive subject.

#18

Helpers serve and labour, while Servants serve with favour

Psalm 127:1

Except the LORD builds the house, they labour in vain that build it: except the LORD keep the city, the watchman waketh but in vain.

Isaiah 12:3

With joy will you drink deeply from the fountain of salvation!

In the scripture above, David the Psalmist was not against the idea of man attempting to build or cease from labouring, neither was he suggesting that the watchmen should neglect their duty. He was simply making us understand the need to yield our work to God and allow Him to control it, rather than relying on our own ability and strength. Otherwise all of our efforts will be in vain.

On the other hand, turning everything over to God does not mean doing nothing and expecting God to do it all for us. You have to do all that you can do. Unless the Lord is in whatever you do and is honoured by it, the whole fibre, or foundation, of your project will crumble and your labour will be in vain. Man may be able to achieve much but without the Lord he has accomplished nothing,

When a man relies on what he can achieve, he has the spirit of a helper. Such a man dedicates a considerable percentage of his time to the wrong thing and ends up achieving nothing.

These people can become so selfish. They are perfectionists, they always believe they can perfect their work. They work and work all day long looking for a perfect touch and in an attempt to do so, they end up ignoring their family and friends, and more importantly their commitment to their calling. As they increasingly search for the magic touch, the less fulfilment and joy they get from their work, because they are not non-dependent on God. It won't be long before the family begin to feel the pain and the man begins to lose his self-esteem.

It is not uncommon for such men to be more loving outside of their home, helping others not out of compassion and love but mostly because of their need to compensate for their overwhelming desire to achieve great things but without God. They become self-critical, believing they are inferior to their peers. They are always trying to prove to the world and more importantly to themselves, that they are somebody. They become so egocentric that they cannot take feedback. They are angry when you give a constructive criticism and sometimes see the feedback as an attack on their person. They engage in hard and continuous exhausting work. They rely on their natural strength as opposed to applying the wisdom of God. When they are given a task, they spend longer time than necessary on it. They work and work and have little return for it.

#18

When you serve and allow God to lead you, your favour will be more than your labour. Servants are relaxed and not stressed, they are not prone to making mistakes. They enjoy serving the Lord.

I remember a young lady in the early years who was part of the janitorial team, as she moved around sweeping, or cleaning the church after the service, she would sing songs of praise to the Lord with her face illuminated with a radiant light and contagious joy. Sometimes she would be the only one cleaning, or would be the last person out, and yet she still sang. You could hear her voice piercing through the air. If the task was not finished on the Sunday night, she would return first thing Monday morning to finish the task.

#19

Helpers eat their seeds, while Servants sow their seeds

Genesis 8:22

While the earth remaineth, seedtime and harvest, and cold and heat, and summer and winter, and day and night shall not cease.

Isaiah 65:14

Behold, my servants shall sing for joy of heart, but ye shall cry for sorrow of heart, and shall howl for vexation of spirit.

Ecclesiastes 11:1-4

Cast thy bread upon the waters: for thou shalt find it after many days. Give a portion to seven, and also to eight; for thou knowest not what evil shall be upon the earth. If the clouds be full of rain, they empty themselves upon the earth: and if the tree fall toward the south, or toward the north, in the place where the tree falleth, there it shall be. He that observeth the wind shall not sow; and he that regardeth the clouds shall not reap.

Psalm 126:5-6

Those who sow in tears shall reap in joy.6 He who continually goes forth weeping, bearing seed for sowing, shall doubtless come again with rejoicing, bringing his sheaves with him.

Too many Christians are still trying to reap where they have never sowed. Or, they are trying to reap a generous harvest when they have sowed sparingly! Many don't understand why they only reap sporadically when their sowing is optional and irregular. Yet the Word of God clearly states that if we want a continual and generous harvest - then we are going to have to sow continually and generously irrespective of whatever state we may be in. We will never change our circumstances until we begin to operate according to the law of sowing and reaping.

God gave us His undisputed and unequivocal assurance that as long as he lives, nature would be predictable and dependable. In other words, he has put a principle in place whereby if we play our part by planting; our seed would multiply. This is one of the main reasons why helpers never see the promises of God manifested in their life. Again and again they attempt to 'stand in faith' and 'believe God' for a generous harvest - yet they have never sowed the amount of seed necessary to obtain that kind of harvest.

God gave us His undisputed and unequivocal assurance that as long as he lives, nature would be predictable and dependable.

Too often they hear from servants of God teaching or preaching on the blessings of prosperity, as promised in the Word of God - and they endeavour to stand in faith and believe God for prosperity - yet they have never followed the instructions on how to obtain the prosperity by sowing faithfully, generously and continually. Most relent after giving once or twice and think to themselves "I can't afford it"- and in doing so never maximise their harvest. They can’t wait until the end of the month. They are broke mid-way through the month and have to rely on their overdraft or they borrow.

#20

Helpers stay on the roundabout, while Servants make a U-turn

Luke 15:11-19

And he said, A certain man had two sons: And the younger of them said to his father, Father, give me the portion of goods that falleth to me. And he divided unto them his living. And not many days after the younger son gathered all together, and took his journey into a far country, and there wasted his substance with riotous living. And when he had spent all, there arose a mighty famine in that land; and he began to be in want. And he went and joined himself to a citizen of that country; and he sent him into his fields to feed swine. And he would fain have filled his belly with the husks that the swine did eat: and no man gave unto him. And when he came to himself, he said, How many hired servants of my father's have bread enough and to spare, and I perish with hunger! I will arise and go to my father, and will say unto him, Father, I have sinned against heaven, and before thee, and am no more worthy to be called thy son: make me as one of thy hired servants.

Some bail out of the church of their planting, sever all relationships, and hurt everybody including their family because of all kinds of reasons and offences. Eventually they realise they have made a grave error but pride and guilt does not allow them to seek repentance and return to their roots. They stay on the roundabout and keep going around and around from one church to another; not finding fulfilment and joy.

> ***You cannot find fulfilment outside the perimeter of the Planting of God for your life.***

A young woman who was genuinely offended by someone decided to move on to another church. Her husband felt otherwise but she pressured him into submission and reluctantly he agreed with her to move church with the whole family. The children who had established themselves in the youth church and formed good relationships, were also reluctant to leave. The family eventually left the church. A few months later, she became disillusioned with this new church. I understand they left the church for another one. The sad thing is that she kept on dragging her husband and children from one church to the other causing them so much pain in the process.

The prodigal son, after all that is said about him at least made a U-turn. He knew where to go when there seemed to be no other way. You cannot find fulfilment outside the perimeter of the Planting of God for your life. A servant recognises the importance of repentance, which is why David said:

Psalm 51:1-11

Have mercy upon me, O God, according to thy lovingkindness: according unto the multitude of thy tender mercies blot out

my transgressions. Wash me thoroughly from mine iniquity, and cleanse me from my sin. For I acknowledge my transgressions: and my sin is ever before me. Against thee, thee only, have I sinned, and done this evil in thy sight: that thou mightest be justified when thou speakest, and be clear when thou judgest. Behold, I was shapen in iniquity; and in sin did my mother conceive me. Behold, thou desirest truth in the inward parts: and in the hidden part thou shalt make me to know wisdom. Purge me with hyssop, and I shall be clean: wash me, and I shall be whiter than snow. Make me to hear joy and gladness; that the bones which thou hast broken may rejoice. Hide thy face from my sins, and blot out all mine iniquities. Create in me a clean heart, O God; and renew a right spirit within me. Cast me not away from thy presence; and take not thy holy spirit from me. Restore unto me the joy of thy salvation; and uphold me with thy free spirit.

David knew he was doomed. Not only did he sleep with another man's wife, he also set this man up for death. He knew the only way was to turn to God. He made a U-turn. He was ready to repent and stay away from the same sin. Many of us don't have a problem in asking for forgiveness from God, but we continuously go back to the same sin.

Helpers stay on the roundabout and go round and round the cycle of sin.

Helpers stay on the roundabout and go around and around the cycle of sin. They eventually lose their joy; that joy that they used to enjoy when they first gave their lives. It won't be long before it begins to reflect in their attitude when they serve. What they used to do with ease before becomes an issue. There is now no sign of the wisdom that people use to admire in them. The focus has become distorted and their sight impaired.

#21

Helpers are worry freaks, while Servants are worry free

Philippians 4:6-7

Do not be anxious about anything, but in every situation, by prayer and petition, with thanksgiving, present your requests to God. And the peace of God, which transcends all understanding, will guard your hearts and your minds in Christ Jesus.

2 Kings 6:14-17

When the servant of the man of God got up and went out early the next morning, an army with horses and chariots had surrounded the city. "Alas, my lord, what shall we do?" the servant asked. "Don't be afraid," the prophet answered. "Those who are with us are more than those who are with them." And Elisha prayed, "O LORD, open his eyes so he may see." Then the LORD opened the servant's eyes, and he looked and saw the hills full of horses and chariots of fire all around Elisha.

According to the scripture, Elisha's servant was so afraid because of what he saw. A city surrounded by enemies fully armed. Rightly so, the reality is that we are likely to be afraid of or worried about something at one time or the other, just like the servant. How we react to the worry is all that matters. Worry is the by-product of fear. The last thing you want is to have too many people in your team who can't deal with their anxiety and worry. They are most likely to slow down the work within your department. They will tell you how that it is not possible to do the job and if care is not taken, they persuade others.

These kind of people are world champion worriers and specialist mind readers. Before you speak they will tell you they know what you want to say. They isolate themselves and don't allow people in their team to get to know them. They are unable to keep friends. Worry will make people like this avoid taking on responsibilities within the team. They always want to do things their way, as a result they put up a barrier to people with authority over them.

Worry freaks have a caretaker attitude, always apologizing even when they are not wrong. They always want to please everyone around them and end up displeasing themselves. When you give them a task, they are worried about making mistakes. They believe something is likely to go wrong. I once served with a young gentleman who would frequently come and ask questions such as; "Did I say the right thing"? "Have I done anything wrong?" "Is the Pastor happy with me?"

When you are free of worry, you are more focused. You become a "go getter" in your department. You are in control of your situation and your time. You put things in perspective and always looking for opportunities. Even when things seem to have gone wrong, a worry free steward looks for a way to turn it around. They are always ready to learn from their mistakes.

#22

Helpers seek after their own thoughts, while Servants seek after their master's heart

2 Kings 5:15-16

Then Naaman and his entire party went back to find the man of God. They stood before him, and Naaman said, "Now I know that there is no God in all the world except in Israel. So please accept a gift from your servant." But Elisha replied, "As surely as the Lord lives, whom I serve, I will not accept any gifts." And though Naaman urged him to take the gift, Elisha refused.

2 Kings 5:20-21

But Gehazi, the servant of Elisha, the man of God, said to himself, "My master should not have let this Aramean get away without accepting any of his gifts. As surely as the Lord lives, I will chase after him and get something from him." So Gehazi set off after Naaman.

It is true, we are created in the image of God, but God created us with our own uniqueness. There is no denying the fact that you are an individual with your own identity. No two people are the same, even the most identical twins. However, when you hang around someone or work with someone for a long time, you are expected to catch the heart of the person. You are expected to know the heart of your master. You should behave in a manner that is similar to the way your master or mentor behaves. When you serve under a leader you seek after the heart of your leader. You watch every one of his steps and emulate everything he does that has brought him success.

Every decision or step you take can either embarrass your head, or cause people to praise him.

Every decision or step you take can either embarrass your head, or cause people to praise him. Gehazi the servant of Elisha sought after his own selfish ends and in the process embarrassed his boss. He brought the name of his master into total disrepute. He brought shame to the house of Elisha. His master had publicly denied the gifts from Naaman, thereby making a statement of his character. When you seek after your own thoughts, you are indirectly saying your master's decisions are not good. You are likely to ignore his instruction believing you can reason better. Gehazi felt Elisha should have taken the gift from Naaman.

When we seek after our own thoughts and not our master's, we become deceitful and hypocritical. We become covetous and dishonourable. We long for those things that are not righteous.

#23

Helpers serve under the dispensation of the Law, while Servants serve under the dispensation of Grace

Isaiah 65:23-24

They shall not labour in vain, nor bring forth for trouble; for they are the seed of the blessed of the LORD, and their offspring with them. And it shall come to pass, that before they call, I will answer; and while they are yet speaking, I will hear.

Hebrews 12:1

Wherefore seeing we also are compassed about with so great a cloud of witnesses, let us lay aside every weight, and the sin which doth so easily beset us, and let us run with patience the race that is set before us.

Sin is one thing that could make a man not enjoy the grace and mercy of God. The children of Israel did not hear from God for 400 years because of their sin. During this period of a closed heaven, they were constantly at war with their enemies, taken as slaves, therefore losing their dignity and freedom. We must be dead to sin, so as to be alive in Christ.

Romans 6:1-11

What shall we say then? Shall we continue in sin, that grace may abound? God forbid. How shall we, that are dead to sin, live any longer therein? Know ye not, that so many of us as were baptized into Jesus Christ were baptized into his death? Therefore we are buried with him by baptism into death: that like as Christ was raised up from the dead by the glory of the Father, even so we also should walk in newness of life. For if we have been planted together in the likeness of his death, we shall be also in the likeness of his resurrection: Knowing this, that our old man is crucified with him, that the body of sin might be destroyed, that henceforth we should not serve sin. For he that is dead is freed from sin. Now if we be dead with Christ, we believe that we shall also live with him: Knowing that Christ being raised from the dead dieth no more; death hath no more dominion over him. For in that he died, he died unto sin once: but in that he liveth, he liveth unto God. Likewise reckon ye also yourselves to be dead indeed unto sin, but alive unto God through Jesus Christ our Lord.

Hebrew 12:1 warns us not to allow sin to easily engulf us. We sometimes assume we are fine as long as we do not fornicate, commit murder or other sins that may carry heavy punishment or are weighty in the sight of man. Little do we realise that God did not categorise sin.

Hebrews 12:1

Wherefore seeing we also are compassed about with so great a cloud of witnesses, let us lay aside every weight, and the sin which doth so easily beset us, and let us run with patience the race that is set before us.

Believe it or not, a sin is a sin. We lie daily, gossip, hurt each other, and don't care about our brothers and sisters feelings. What about that pen you took from your office without asking your employer, and the overnight stay in the house of your boyfriend only to show up in the Church to serve the following morning? You lift up unholy hands in worship, polluting the altar of God.

We do all this and expect the grace of God to abound. It is clear we open ourselves up to be judged according to the law. We are in danger of creating a closed heaven over our family, business, church or other part of our life. The truth is that sin separates us from the love of God.

Romans 6:1 (NIV)

What shall we say, then? Shall we go on sinning so that grace may increase?

When you walk in sin, it robs you of your joy. Everything becomes impossible. Nothing works no matter how much you try. You suppress the truth and become insensitive. You become impure in your thinking and blind to spiritual truth. There is a continual lust for power. Your conscience is seared with hot iron, and you find yourself in a constant state of confusion, loneliness and guilt. You contaminate your vision and purpose.

#24

Helpers serve with answers, while Servants serve with questions

Numbers 13:17-20

Then Moses sent them to spy out the land of Canaan, and said to them, "Go up this way into the South, and go up to the mountains, and see what the land is like: whether the people who dwell in it are strong or weak, few or many; whether the land they dwell in is good or bad; whether the cities they inhabit are like camps or strongholds; whether the land is rich or poor; and whether there are forests there or not. Be of good courage. And bring some of the fruit of the land." Now the time was the season of the first ripe grapes.

In the scriptures above Moses gave twelve leaders an assignment to spy on the city of Canaan. He gave them a set of objectives:

⇒ To check what the land was like

⇒ To check on the population and on the strength of the inhabitants of the city

⇒ To check if the country was rich and to bring back evidence of its wealth

Ten of the twelve came back with negative results. They focused on all the negatives of the land despite accepting that the land was rich. They even brought back fruits from the land. They came back focusing on the problems rather than first analysing it and working out how they could overcome the problems. They couldn't see the way in or out of the city. In their opinion, they couldn't occupy the city. It was a no go area because of their inability to thoroughly look beyond the problems. They returned to their master with the hope that he would find solution to the problems they identified.

Negative people ask questions rather than provide answers to questions.

You must learn to not only identify a problem, but find a solution to the problem before you approach your group, your leader or even your family. When you feed people with the negatives you create an atmosphere of fear and despair. You instantly affect the mood of the people and damage any enthusiasm they may have.

I have heard of people who received negative news and either fainted, had a heart attack or worst still dropped dead. A man who was to have a simple routine operation was told by a friend that people can die on the operating table. As he was being wheeled into the theatre, he had a heart attack and died even before the operation as a result of the negative statement made by his friend. The friend gave him the negatives of an operation but not the positives. He did not tell him of the many millions of success stories there are. He rather focused on the few negatives and ended up killing his friend.

Negative people ask questions, rather than provide answers to questions. They are a burden to their team members. They create a mess whenever they are given a task and leave others to clear up after them. They are not creative. They only see things from one perspective. They do not multi-task, they only do the basics.

> ***Servants solve problems; they look for solutions to problems, as opposed to creating problems.***

Today's Leaders have little or no time to find answers to every question. That is why they have other people around them who will provide the answers to questions, rather than only ask them. Presidents and Prime Ministers will have a cabinet with a Minister responsible for each portfolio. He or she expects the Minister to resolve the problems within their area and not vice versa.

When you show up at the desk of your leader, you must not only show up with the problems. You show up with the problems or questions in one hand and the strategy to solve in the other hand. By so doing, you are making the job of your leader easier. He either approves the answers or makes some adjustment to the answers you have provided.

21st Century Leaders like Matthew Ashimolowo have a helicopter view. Their main task is to come up with great ideas and turn it over to the team around them to run with the idea and make it happen. Simply put; they ask the questions, you provide the answers. In the twenty or more years I have served with Pastor Matthew, I have learnt not to go to him with a problem without presenting a solution at the same time.

Servants solve problems; they look for solutions to problems, as opposed to creating problems.

#25

Helpers serve according to their own understanding, while Servants serve with God's understanding

Proverbs 3:5-6

Trust in the Lord with all thine heart; and lean not unto thine own understanding. In all thy ways acknowledge him, and he shall direct thy paths.

According to Collins, The English dictionary, the word "lean" means to rest or cause to rest against a support. Sometimes we forget we have limitations and don't lean on God. We tend to rely on our intellect, our education, our achievements, and our experience of life more than we rely on God. Our experience of life can never be enough to deal with the affairs of life.

Life is sometimes like a biscuit, you cannot tell where it will break. You may be so sure that you are on the right track to bringing a solution to a task but end up discovering that you have missed out on some key information. The truth is, a son cannot have as much rags as the father. The one who made us has a better solution than we do.

Is this passage saying that understanding is bad? After all several scriptures talk about the benefits of having understanding. The answer is No. One scripture says, in all our getting, "get understanding". So if the scripture encourages us to get understanding, why can't we lean on it? What the scripture says is that we should not lean on our own understanding but on God's understanding.

When we lean on our own understanding, we are prone to stumbling or falling. We become unstable and insecure. We are like a tree without a firm root which could be blown away at the slightest wind.

The Prophet Isaiah made us understand that our human understanding is so limited; and cannot be compared to that of the Lord. When we lean on our own understanding, we are prone to stumbling or falling. We become unstable and insecure. We are like a tree without a firm root which could be blown away by the slightest wind.

Isaiah 55:8-9

For my thoughts are not your thoughts, neither are your ways my ways, saith the Lord. For as the heavens are higher than the earth, so are my ways higher than your ways, and my thoughts than your thoughts.

Proverb 5:6 says we should trust in the Lord with all out heart. You can only trust in Him if you acknowledge Him. When you apply your heart to what you do and acknowledge Him, you can be sure of success. When you serve with all your heart, He will direct your paths and your footsteps. You will reach decisions without any stress. When others are panicking, you will be cool in your decision, making your decisions stress free. When you apply all your heart to what God has committed into your hand, it helps you to have a closer relationship with Him and He will in turn pay close attention to what you are doing.

Those who lean on their understanding rely on their strength and ability. It's all about what they can achieve and not about what God can achieve through them. True servants serve with the wisdom from above and seek God's insight and understanding. Every decision they take is ordered of God and not based on their understanding. They trust in God when they don't understand. When you yield everything to him you let go of your pride, your intellect, your knowledge and ability. ***Proverb 16:25*** says, ***"There is a way that appears to be right to man but in the end leads to death.***

Helpers harbour a belief that nothing will work if they are not there; they are theorists and very good propagandists. They believe they are smarter and wiser than everyone. They reject words of wisdom and try to convince everyone that their theory or idea is the best. They are authoritative and find it difficult to comprehend other people's ideas. In a way, they see themselves as being omnipotent.

#26

Helpers operate an open-mouthed policy, while Servants operate a closed-mouthed policy

Ephesians 4:29

Let no corrupt communication proceed out of your mouth, but that which is good to the use of edifying, that it may minister grace unto the hearers.

Mark 9:9-10 (NIV)

As they were coming down the mountain, Jesus gave them orders not to tell anyone what they had seen until the Son of Man had risen from the dead. They kept the matter to themselves, discussing what "rising from the dead" meant. news

Genesis 9:20-25

And Noah began to bean husbandman, and he planted a vineyard: And he drank of the wine, and was drunken; and he was uncovered within his tent. And Ham, the father of Canaan, saw the nakedness of his father, and told his two brethren without. And Shem and Japheth took a garment, and laid] it upon both their shoulders, and went backward, and covered the nakedness of their father; and their faces were

backward, and they saw not their father's nakedness. And Noah awoke from his wine, and knew what his younger son had done unto him. And he said, Cursed be Canaan; a servant of servants shall he be unto his brethren.

Many views have been aired about why Noah cursed Canaan the first son of Ham. Some scholars believe Ham must have done more than just see his father's nakedness, hence his anger towards him even to his generation. I will not try to explain why but I would like to point out the fact that Ham exposed his father.

He uncovered his father's nakedness. When anyone is naked they become vulnerable. Noah was in a vulnerable state. Ham was quick to tell others about his father's problems. He saw his father naked and passed out in his tent, under the influence of alcohol and walked away from him. He allowed passers-by, neighbours or friends to see the shame of his father rather than try to first cover him up. Not only did he leave him to his shame, he also invited his two brothers to see the nakedness of their father.

As a servant, when we see our brother sin or fall, we don't go about spreading the news, instead, we help the brother to come out of the sin by praying for him. Ham should have covered his father's nakedness. We must not forget that nakedness, as in the story of Adam and Eve, symbolises exposing sin.

Ham showed disrespect and disregard to his father Noah, who was the head of the family. Ham's action is representative of gossiping, backbiting and magnifying the fault of his father. Ham tried to lure his two brothers to also follow his own footsteps but they refused. They understood the position of their father as the prophet of the house and the head of the family, an elder and also

They slaughter their brethren on the altar of gossip; have their Pastor for breakfast, their Deacons for lunch and the Pastor's wife for dinner.

the authority over their heads. They understood that their father is human and can make mistakes. They understood it is not everything you see or hear, that you share or talk about. They knew the right thing to do was to avoid seeing the shortfall of their father, that was why they turned their back and walked backwards to cover him.

People like Ham say all the negatives about their leaders, or their brethren. They breathe negative, see negative and act negative. They go about knocking those who are in the position of authority, or in the organisation they work. They sit with scorners and murmurers and become the local radio of the organisation, broadcasting negative news about the brethren. They slaughter their brethren on the altar of gossip; have their Pastor for breakfast, their Deacons for lunch and the Pastor's wife for dinner.

#27

Helpers are second to none, while Servants are second to one

Esther 5:9-11

Then went Haman forth that day joyful and with a glad heart: but when Haman saw Mordecai in the king's gate, that he stood not up, nor moved for him, he was full of indignation against Mordecai. Nevertheless Haman refrained himself: and when he came home, he sent and called for his friends, and Zeresh his wife. And Haman told them of the glory of his riches, and the multitude of his children, and all the things wherein the king had promoted him, and how he had advanced him above the princes and servants of the king.

Esther 1:10

On the seventh day, when King Xerxes was in high spirits from wine, he commanded the seven eunuchs who served him—Mehuman, Biztha, Harbona, Bigtha, Abagtha, Zethar and Karkas—to bring before him Queen Vashti, wearing her royal crown, in order to display her beauty to the people and nobles, for she was lovely to look at. But when the attendants delivered the king's command, Queen Vashti refused to come. Then the king became furious and burned with anger.

The name Vashti in Hebrew, is derived from the Persian words for beautiful woman. The Bible described Vashti as a beautiful woman who was lovely to look at. I believe that was why the King was going to show her off.

> ***A second to none person demands respect and recognition at all cost. They decorate their names with their accolades and take pride in their titles. You dear not call them without their titles otherwise they get angry.***

Don't get me wrong, I am not insinuating that the practice of a King parading his Queen in front of drunken men is right, but let us for the sake of this argument accept that this practice is right. We wouldn't be wrong to say that Vashti arrogated herself over the rules of the Kingdom. You can argue Vashti refused to be paraded because she valued herself more than she should. She put herself on a high pedestal. She became too conscious of her beauty and thought she was better than everyone else. She placed her own interest above the interest of the Kingdom. Her Class and status was more important.

Sometimes we look down on other people because they are different from us. We see ourselves as superior to people from other cultures. In the case of Vashti, it was her beauty and her status. The scripture make us understand that she also gave a banquet for the women in the royal palace of the King. She was more concerned about her status and her host. Why should she leave her guests? She felt her reputation was at stake.

When you see yourself being second to none, you are susceptible to undermining the authority of your organisation with your actions. When you ignore the instructions from your leaders and humiliate them in the process, you are a helper.

Haman, irrespective of his position as the second most important guy in the kingdom – or so he thought, could not hide his disdain towards Mordecai. He became so conscious of his great power and influence in the kingdom, and felt he was above everyone. He was so enraged because Mordecai would not stand up or bow down to him.

A second to none person demands respect and recognition at all cost. They decorate their names with their accolades and take pride in their titles. You dare not call them without their titles otherwise they get angry.

They are self-centred and everything must always be about them. They don't mind if their action brings the church or the organisation into disrepute, or bring the Pastor to his or her feet. They think more highly of themselves, major on the minors and minor on the majors. ***(Romans 14:16-18).*** On the other hand servants think soberly of themselves ***(Romans 12:3&16)***, give preference to others and honour the desires of others above theirs ***(Romans 121:0)***.

#28

Helpers are hole diggers, while Servants are bridge builders

Esther 3:1-3

After these things King Ahasuerus promoted Haman, the son of Hammedatha the Agagite, and advanced him and set his seat above all the princes who were with him. And all the king's servants who were within the king's gate bowed and paid homage to Haman, for so the king had commanded concerning him. But Mordecai would not bow or pay homage.

Esther 5:14-15

Then his wife Zeresh and all his friends said to him, "Let a gallows be made, fifty cubits high, and in the morning suggest to the king that Mordecai be hanged on it; then go merrily with the king to the banquet." And the thing pleased Haman; so he had the gallows made.

This is similar to the last one. Haman was said to have been hanged on the same gallows that he prepared for Mordecai. Rather than his wife and friends helping him to understand his folly, they dug a hole into which he eventually fell and died. Rather than build a bridge for him to cross and overcome his hatred and anger against Mordecai, they encouraged him by adding more fire. Haman's wife and friends told him to build a gallows so Mordecai could be hung on it. Your friend can either help you to righteousness, or onto total destruction.

We saw a similar spirit in Judas. His action was tantamount to digging a hole into which Jesus Christ fell. He engineered Jesus' downfall, that led Him to His death, by selling Him for thirty pieces of silver.

Esther1:16-20

Then Memukan replied in the presence of the king and the nobles, "Queen Vashti has done wrong, not only against the king but also against all the nobles and the peoples of all the provinces of King Xerxes. For the queen's conduct will become known to all the women, and so they will despise their husbands and say, 'King Xerxes commanded Queen Vashti to be brought before him, but she would not come.' This very day the Persian and Median women of the nobility who have heard about the queen's conduct will respond to all the king's nobles in the same way. There will be no end of disrespect and discord. "Therefore, if it pleases the king, let him issue a royal decree and let it be written in the laws of Persia and Media, which cannot be repealed, that Vashti is never again to enter the presence of King Xerxes. Also let the king give her royal position to someone else who is better than she. Then when the king's edict is proclaimed throughout all his vast realm, all the women will respect their husbands, from the least to the greatest."

#28

In the scripture above, we see how King Xerxes' friends and right hand men gave him bad advice. He was advised to get rid of his wife and arrange a contest to replace her. Xerxes was made to face the consequence of his actions.

> ***Hole diggers would sit with you, eat with you, laugh with you and give you a kiss of death.***

1 Kings 12:8-11(NIV)

But Rehoboam rejected the advice the elders gave him and consulted the young men who had grown up with him and were serving him. He asked them, "What is your advice? How should we answer these people who say to me, 'Lighten the yoke your father put on us'?" The young men who had grown up with him replied, "These people have said to you, 'Your father put a heavy yoke on us, but make our yoke lighter.' Now tell them, 'My little finger is thicker than my father's waist. My father laid on you a heavy yoke; I will make it even heavier. My father scourged you with whips; I will scourge you with scorpions.'"

After the death of his father, Rehoboam rejected the advice of the elders who had served his father Solomon for several years and sought the advice of his friends. They dug a hole with their stupid advice, which led to Rehoboam's downfall.

When we see our brother or sister on the road to destruction, we should do everything to help them to follow the right way. **Hole diggers will sit with you, eat with you, laugh with you and give you a kiss of death.** They make you believe they are with you in times of trouble and knowingly give you bad advice.

They encourage you to revolt or rise up against your leaders and abandon you when you run into trouble.

This reminds me of one of my classmates in secondary school. He was always behind all kinds of trouble in the school. He would lead the way to commit all kinds of atrocities and denied knowledge of the sin. I remember a particular incidence when he and a number of students went to the corn farm of one of the village farmers, for unauthorised harvesting. The boys were full of fear because of the consequences of their action if they were caught. He was so reassuring they forgot the consequence in a jiffy. When the farmer showed up, this boy was the first to run and was never caught. He denied knowledge of the operation and left the rest of the boys to face the punishment. They thought they had an ally but they were quick to find out otherwise.

Such people can be so trustworthy and very friendly and yet they are very contagious. They are like a green snake under the green grass. They are so convincing everyone believes them. They dig holes with the hope that a colleague will fall into them. They set up gallows and block wells because they covet other people's position and blessings. They are full of jealousy and never content.

#29

Helpers are takers, while Servants are givers

Acts 5:1-2

But a certain man named Ananias, with Sapphira his wife, sold a possession. And he kept back part of the proceeds, his wife also being aware of it, and brought a certain part and laid it at the apostles' feet.

Servants, give their time, energy, their money, even themselves to the furtherance of the vision of the organisation. Helpers give with a fisted hand, while servants give with an open hand.

Acts 20:35

I have shewed you all things, how that so labouring ye ought to support the weak, and to remember the words of the Lord Jesus, how he said, It is more blessed to give than to receive.

If someone shows up now in the midst of about one hundred people and announces he wants to hand out a £50 note to everyone, you don't have to be a betting man to conclude that ninety-nine out of the one hundred people are likely to accept the gift. Let us do the reverse. If someone shows up in the midst of the same hundred people and requests to be a given £50 note, you wouldn't be wrong to say perhaps one out of the one hundred people would reciprocate. Why is it so? It is simply because it is easier to receive than to give.

A rich man wants to continue to be rich. He thinks giving out of the little, or much he has could hinder him. When you give, you are obeying God's command. Luke, who was credited as the author of the book of Acts wrote to remind us of Jesus' command for us to give. Hebrew 13:16 talks about us not neglecting to do good and to share what we have because such sacrifice is pleasing to God. ***Do not neglect to do good and to share what you have, for such sacrifices are pleasing to God. Hebrews 13:16.***

When you give, it is a sign of respect to God your Father. You are only trying to be like Him. The supreme argument for giving is God Himself. He gave the biggest gift anyone can give. His only begotten Son. ***2 Corinthians 2:9*** couldn't have been clearer. He gave an account of Jesus Christ; how ***"He was rich, yet for our sakes He became poor, that you through His poverty we might become rich".***

We are always of the opinion that we won't have enough for the future when we give. **Our wallets are the battle grounds between 'release' and 'hold', it is often the last stronghold to fall to God's rule and command.** Little do we realise that when we empty our wallets, it gets refilled beyond measure. When you sow seeds, or give sacrificially, for the benefit of others, particularly to those around you who are in need, you are indirectly doing yourself a favour. Giving provokes God to perform on behalf of the giver.

#29

> ***Our wallets are the battle ground between 'release' and 'hold', it is often the last stronghold to fall to God's rule and command.***

Those who take and not give are tight fisted. They only came to help and not to serve. They pledge and never fulfil their pledges. They are the first to rush out when a special offering is called; happy to receive the blessing of the Pastor. When you argue with your wife or your husband, when there is any need to be part of a fund raising initiative in your church for a just course, you are a taker. When you argue whether the tithe should be 10% before or after tax, you are a taker or better, still a helper.

#30

Helpers are bench-warmers, while Servants are bench-fillers

Matthew 28:16-20

Then the eleven disciples went to Galilee, to the mountain where Jesus had told them to go. When they saw him, they worshiped him; but some doubted. Then Jesus came to them and said, "All authority in heaven and on earth has been given to me. Therefore go and make disciples of all nations, baptizing them in the name of the Father and of the Son and of the Holy Spirit, and teaching them to obey everything I have commanded you. And surely I am with you always, to the very end of the age."

John 1:35-42 (NIV)

The next day John was there again with two of his disciples. When he saw Jesus passing by, he said, "Look, the Lamb of God!" When the two disciples heard him say this, they followed Jesus. Turning around, Jesus saw them following and asked, "What do you want?" They said, "Rabbi" (which means "Teacher"), "where are you staying?" "Come," he replied, "and you will see." So they went and saw where he was staying, and

they spent that day with him. It was about four in the afternoon. Andrew, Simon Peter's brother, was one of the two who heard what John had said and who had followed Jesus. The first thing Andrew did was to find his brother Simon and tell him, "We have found the Messiah" (that is, the Christ). And he brought him to Jesus. Jesus looked at him and said, "You are Simon son of John. You will be called Cephas" (which, when translated, is Peter).The next day Jesus decided to leave for Galilee. Finding Philip, he said to him, "Follow me." Philip, like Andrew and Peter, was from the town of Bethsaida. Philip found Nathanael and told him, "We have found the one Moses wrote about in the Law, and about whom the prophets also wrote—Jesus of Nazareth, the son of Joseph."

John 12:20-24 (NIV)

Now there were some Greeks among those who went up to worship at the festival. They came to Philip, who was from Bethsaida in Galilee, with a request. "Sir," they said, "we would like to see Jesus." Philip went to tell Andrew; Andrew and Philip in turn told Jesus.

There are many examples in the Bible of disciples bringing others to Jesus. A true servant of Christ must have a burning desire to populate the Kingdom of God by bringing people to Christ, just as Andrew and Phillip did. The scripture makes us understand in John 1:40 that the first thing Andrew did after meeting with Jesus Christ was to find his brother Simon Peter. He told him, "we have found the Messiah". Andrew used the word 'we' and not 'I'. He was not going to enjoy his new found life alone. He was determined to share it with his brother.

Many of us today can't be bothered if others perish as long as we are fine. There are very few soul winners in the house today, many of us warm the bench rather than fill the bench. We blame the Pastor and the Leadership of the church if the church is not growing numerically. We forget it is up to us to make it happen. We often forget the Commandment of Christ Jesus in Mark 28:19-20. This Commandment was not directed to Pastors and leaders alone, but to every one of us. No wonder the Bible says in Matthew 9:37 that the harvest is plenteous, but the labourers are few'. Jesus wants us to go and reach out to the sinners and the unbelievers and bring them to Him as Andrew and Phillip did.

How ironic that the first person Andrew found was his own brother. He did this because it is easier and natural to reach out to your family, your friend, your colleagues and the people around you. A simple but effective survey was once carried out in my local church by way of a raise of hands. The question was asked how they became members of the church. Over 75% said they came to the church either through a friend or a family member.

Of the twelve Apostles of Jesus, Andrew was there with his brother Simon Peter, so also was James with his brother John. It is believed the foursome were partners in a fishing business. They brought each other to Christ. There are other accounts of Andrew in the Bible bringing people to Christ. He brought a boy with two fishes and five loaves of bread in John 6:8-13. He also teamed up with Philip to bring some Greeks to Jesus who wanted to meet him in John 12:20-22.

The story was told of a young Pastor who was informed by his Bishop how badly he was doing with his work. The supervisor told him, "Only one person has been added to your Parish in a year, and he is only a boy." The Pastor was so heartbroken and disturbed. One day as he knelt down to pray, the little convert touched his shoulder and he turned around, the boy said, "Pastor, do you think I could become a preacher or missionary some day?" The Pastor in a soft voice replied; "yes you can" and he encouraged him to pray about it and seek the face of God.

The little boy whose name was Robert Moffit truly became a Preacher who was destined to open Africa to the Gospel of Christ. Years later, whilst Pastor Moffit was speaking in his church in London, a young doctor heard him say, "I have seen in the morning sun the smoke of a thousand villages where no missionary has ever been." The young doctor, deeply moved by Moffit's message, was none other than David Livingstone. In 1840, he sailed for Africa where he laboured for Jesus for more than three decades. David Livingstone was later to bring Christianity to some parts of Southern Africa. This was all possible because of the commitment and faithfulness of a Parish Pastor who was only able to convert just a little boy in a year.

It is not about the number of people you convert in a year; it is about playing your part and leaving the rest to God. Heaven will rejoice even for one soul.

Servants are naturally people bringers. They are "fishermen" they understand the great command of God to evangelise the world. On the other hand, **helpers sit on the fence, critical of the church; expelling as opposed to redeeming the time.** They are full of excuses. They warm the bench so much they don't feel the heat they are generating.

#31

Helpers disrespect the anointing of their master, while Servants embrace the anointing of their master

1 Samuel 24:1-7

After Saul returned from pursuing the Philistines, he was told, "David is in the Desert of EnGedi." So Saul took three thousand able young men from all Israel and set out to look for David and his men near the Crags of the Wild Goats. He came to the sheep pens along the way; a cave was there, and Saul went in to relieve himself. David and his men were far back in the cave. The men said, "This is the day the Lord spoke of when he said to you, 'I will give your enemy into your hands for you to deal with as you wish.'" Then David crept up unnoticed and cut off a corner of Saul's robe. Afterward, David was conscience-stricken for having cut off a corner of his robe. He said to his men, "The Lord forbid that I should do such a thing to my master, the Lord's anointed, or lay my hand on him; for he is the anointed of the Lord." With these words David sharply rebuked his men and did not allow them to attack Saul. And Saul left the cave and went his way.

David respected the anointing upon the life of Saul. He refused to harm him even though he had the opportunity to do so on a handful of occasions. He understood God was not joking when he said in 1 Chronicles 16:22 “Do not touch My anointed ones, And do My prophets no harm”. He recognised the anointing on King Saul. He knew he was a man anointed by God irrespective of Saul’s misdemeanours.

David had two opportunities to kill King Saul, and on both occasions he refused to kill him, or allow his men to do so.

In 1 Samuel 31:3-5, Saul’s armour bearer recognised the anointing on Saul and he refused his offer to kill him to avoid the enemy doing so. He went further to fall on his own sword when he saw Saul fall on his.

2 Samuel 16:5-8

Now when King David came to Bahurim, there was a man from the family of the house of Saul, whose name was Shimei the son of Gera, coming from there. He came out, cursing continuously as he came. And he threw stones at David and at all the servants of King David. And all the people and all the mighty men were on his right hand and on his left. Also Shimei said thus when he cursed: “Come out! Come out! You bloodthirsty man, you rogue! The Lord has brought upon you all the blood of the house of Saul, in whose place you have reigned; and the Lord has delivered the kingdom into the hand of Absalom your son. So now you are caught in your own evil, because you are a bloodthirsty man!”

Shimei a relative of King Saul whom David replaced as King disrespected the anointing upon the life of David when he was running away from his son Absalom. He mocked him, forgetting he was the anointed of God. He harboured so much hatred for David because he ousted his relative. He couldn't forgive David and was looking for a way to revenge. He seized the opportunity the moment it showed up, thereby making the greatest mistake of his life. He decided to kick David while he was down on the ground. What a cowardly attitude.

Jesus Christ also experienced similar disrespect at Calvary by one of the two thieves he was crucified with. He was also mocked by the soldiers and the rulers saying; "If you are the King of the Jews, save yourself."

A helper in this context can be so rude and condescending. They have uncultured tongues and untamed body language.

Servants always recognise that they operate under the anointing of their master, leader or their Pastor and not their own anointing. They remain obedient to the vision of the house. They don't set out with their own vision, believing they can do it better than their Pastor.

A helper in this context can be so rude and condescending. They have uncultured tongues and untamed body language. Anger resides in their bosom. They embrace and tango with pride. They are unforgiving and hold grudges, bottling offenders up in their mind. They are most likely to seek revenge if a colleague offends them. They have removed the word humility from their dictionaries. They always struggle to submit their will to that of the Lord.

#32

Helpers focus on the obstacles, while Servants focus on the objectives

2 Kings 6:14-17

Therefore he sent horses and chariots and a great army there, and they came by night and surrounded the city. And when the servant of the man of God arose early and went out, there was an army, surrounding the city with horses and chariots. And his servant said to him, "Alas, my master! What shall we do?" So he answered, "Do not fear, for those who are with us are more than those who are with them." And Elisha prayed, and said, "Lord, I pray, open his eyes that he may see." Then the Lord opened the eyes of the young man, and he saw. And behold, the mountain was full of horses and chariots of fire all around Elisha.

Numbers 13:30-33

Then Caleb quieted the people before Moses, and said, "Let us go up at once and take possession, for we are well able to overcome it." But the men who had gone up with him said, "We are not able to go up against the people, for they are stronger than we." And they gave the children of Israel a bad

report of the land which they had spied out, saying, "The land through which we have gone as spies is a land that devours its inhabitants, and all the people whom we saw in it are men of great stature. There we saw the giants (the descendants of Anak came from the giants); and we were like grasshoppers in our own sight, and so we were in their sight."

Every organisation has more people who focus more on the problems, rather than the main objectives of the organisation or church. All they see are the challenges. They magnify the challenges and in the process forget the overall objectives. Their favourite serving tool is a magnifier.

The story was told of a young associate Pastor who was asked by the Senior Pastor to check how many people were in the service. He came back and told the Senior Pastor the church is "half empty". The Senior Pastor asked another associate Pastor the same thing; he came back with a different report. He said the church "is half full". Ten of the twelve tribes who were sent out saw the goodness of the land but did not believe in the power of God. They saw the difficulties, the strength of their enemies and the fortified cities and their hearts melted in fear. They were intimidated by the size and strength of their enemies. They allowed their fears to reduce them to mere grasshoppers, undermining their abilities and most importantly who they were in the Lord. The ten spies were paralysed and demoralised with fear. They took God out of the situation and allowed the obstacles to blind their eyes and close their hearts. They lost sight of the great God behind them and jumped from fear into presumption. They tried to overcome their enemies by their own power.

In the second scripture, Caleb and Joshua were full of courage and deep conviction. They did not ignore the presence of a strong obstacle nor deny the strength of their enemies, but they trusted in the power of God. Caleb and Joshua stood against the negative influence of the majority. They were not influenced by fear. They were spiritually and physically strong. At the age of 85, when other men had already retired, Caleb conquered the mountain of giants. His faith in God reduced the giants of the land into grasshoppers. He saw that the real giant was God and the real grasshoppers were their enemies.

Their favourite serving tool is a magnifier.

Caleb and Joshua stood as spiritual giants among the generation of grasshoppers and pigmies. Caleb and Joshua were not pigmies in their own eyes because they knew that God was residing in their hearts.

#33

Helpers walk away from their master's instructions, while Servants follow through their master's instructions

Genesis 24:10-11

Then the servant took ten of his master's camels and departed, for all his master's goods were in his hand. And he arose and went to Mesopotamia, to the city of Nahor. And he made his camels kneel down outside the city by a well of water at evening time, the time when women go out to draw water.

What a bizarre errand. Abraham sent his servant to go get a wife for his son Isaac. In his human understanding, he could have easily disobeyed, amended or experimented with his master's instructions, considering the unusual nature of the errand. He could have convinced himself this can't be right. Abraham's servant followed his master's instruction to the letter. Servants will act upon every instruction to fulfil the vision. They remain faithful despite difficulties, struggles or a lack of resources. They are subject to their master's authority regardless of differences in opinion. They never demand their own way.

I have learnt to never question my Pastor's instructions, even though it may not make sense to me at the time. Given time, it becomes clearer why he gave the instruction. Many times in the scriptures, God will give instructions that make you think, can this be God? For example He told Hosea to take a prostitute as a wife.

Hosea 1:2

When the LORD first began speaking to Israel through Hosea, he said to him, "Go and marry a prostitute, so that some of her children will be conceived in prostitution. This will illustrate how Israel has acted like a prostitute by turning against the LORD and worshiping other gods."

God instructed Jonah to go to Nineveh to preach to the city for repentance but Jonah went on another journey in rebellion to God's instruction. He walked away from his Master's instruction, rather than follow it through. Just like Jonah, we may feel the instructions we have been given are way too hard, so we don't try. Sometimes we may feel the instruction is irrelevant, unnecessary or meaningless. We begin to adjust, rewrite or ignore it. When we do this, we do it with the spirit of a helper.

Your act of disobedience affects the people around you, just as Jonah's actions affected those who were in the boat with him. The storm came because of Jonah and it almost caused the death of everyone in the boat. Just one Jonah in your ship is enough to sink your boat. It is important we do not become a candidate for a downward path and therefore highly unlikely to hear the voice of the Lord just like Jonah. He was fast asleep when God was speaking to him through the storm. He took the unbelievers around him to wake him up from his slumber.

When you operate with a spirit like this, your prayer life becomes erratic and sometimes come to a sudden stop. You no longer feel you need to pray because you know it all and can do it all. Jonah had to be reminded by the Captain of the ship of his need to rise and pray. Jonah's disobedience has caused his heart to be seared with hot iron.

Jonah 1:6

"So the captain approached him and said, "How is it that you are sleeping? Get up, call on your god. Perhaps your god will be concerned about us so that we will not perish."

Jonah 1:1-3

The Lord gave this message to Jonah son of Amittai: "Get up and go to the great city of Nineveh. Announce my judgment against it because I have seen how wicked its eople are." But Jonah got up and went in the opposite direction to get away from the Lord. He went down to the port of Joppa, where he found a ship leaving for Tarshish. He bought a ticket and went on board, hoping to escape from the Lord by sailing to Tarshish.

#34

Helpers think God owes them, while Servants see themselves as debtors to God

Romans 1:14

I am a debtor both to Greeks and to barbarians, both to wise and to unwise.

Servants believe serving God is a way of paying their debt. On the other hand, helpers constantly demand that God "pay" them their own way and if it doesn't happen they stop serving.

Luke 17:5-10 (Amplified)

Will any man of you who has a servant plowing or tending sheep say to him when he has come in from the field, Come at once and take your place at the table? Will he not instead tell him, Get my supper ready and gird yourself and serve me while I eat and drink; then afterward you yourself shall eat and drink? Is he grateful and does he praise the servant because he did what he was ordered to do? Even so on your part, when you have done everything that was assigned and commanded you, say, We are unworthy servants [possessing no merit, for we have not gone beyond our obligation]; we have [merely] done what was our duty to do.

This parable talks about how our service can never be adequate with God. We can never serve God enough irrespective of how many hours, days, months or years we put into our service to Him. We can never pay back the debt we owe God or surpass His love, grace and blessing upon our lives. We must always remember as we serve God, it was because of His grace and the precious blood His son shed, that qualifies us for His Kingdom. We are called solely because of His love. Otherwise we would not be worthy to even stand in His courtyard.

He paid the price for you and me. How then can we ever think He owes us to the point that we can claim credit for the work we do in His kingdom? Our attitude must always be that of a humble and grateful servant, one who understands that our service to God does not necessarily compel Him to pay us accordingly. If He does, it will be in His own time and out of His large heart.

As a servant and as we serve the LORD, we must remember we are only doing what we are commanded to do or rather, simply performing our duty. To think that God owes us is the pinnacle of stupidity and self-importance or arrogance. Does it mean God owes us anything because we obey Him, by paying our tithe, don't commit fornication or adultery? Far from it, He is God on His own and He does things according to His purpose and what pleases him. Phillipians 2:13 (NLT).

Job was described as a man who was blameless and upright, a man who feared God and yet he lost everything that was dear to him; his children and his business even his health.

Job was so into God that even his wife believed that God owed her husband. She questioned why God's payment method was to destroy her family. She asked Job to curse God and die. Job's answer to her was that she "speaks as a foolish woman." Job knew God owed him nothing and refused to be coerced by his emotional wife, who was acting on her impulse and pain.

Paul the Apostle was another good example of a servant who understood his responsibilities to God. He never forgot how Jesus saved him on the way to Damascus. He was committed to serving God. He knew he owed God his life rather than God owing him anything. He was determined to give that life back to Him if necessary.

To think that God owes us is the pinnacle of stupidity and self-importance or arrogance.

1 Peter 1:18-19

Forasmuch as ye know that ye were not redeemed with corruptible things, as silver and gold, from your vain conversation received by tradition from your fathers; But with the precious blood of Christ, as of a lamb without blemish and without spot:

In 2 Samuel 9:1-9, the scripture reveals how David showed kindness to Mephibosheth, the grandson of David and son of Jonathan. Mephibosheth became crippled while he was being taken away when his grandfather's house was under siege and ambush. He since lived in a remote village, living a lowly life and in abject poverty; struggling to make ends meet.

Despite his disability, David restored him to glory and gave him everything that belonged to his grandfather. He let Mephibosheth wine and dine at the Kings table with servants working on his behalf. In chapter 16, Mephibosheth turned against David when he was in trouble. He thought David owed him and felt it was payback time. He coveted the throne of David and couldn't help but say to himself in verse 3; "today the house of Israel will restore the Kingdom of my father to me.'" He was a pretender and was never satisfied with the kindness of David. Such people don't know how to say thank you. It does not matter what you do for them, they will never show appreciation.

2 Samuel 16:1-4

When David was a little past the top of the mountain, there was Ziba the servant of Mephibosheth, who met him with a couple of saddled donkeys, and on them two hundred loaves of bread, one hundred clusters of raisins, one hundred summer fruits, and a skin of wine. And the king said to Ziba, "What do you mean to do with these?" So Ziba said, "The donkeys are for the king's household to ride on, the bread and summer fruit for the young men to eat, and the wine for those who are faint in the wilderness to drink." Then the king said, "And where is your master's son?" And Ziba said to the king, "Indeed he is staying in Jerusalem, for he said, 'Today the house of Israel will restore the kingdom of my father to me.'" So the king said to Ziba, "Here, all that belongs to Mephibosheth is yours." And Ziba said, "I humbly bow before you, that I may find favor in your sight, my lord, O king!"

People who think God owes them will moan when their breakthroughs are delayed. They can't handle pressure. They fall apart and become blasphemous. They speak in a derogatory way of God and His Words. They forget the time when things were so good and put their success down to their strength, their own making or sheer luck. They are highly emotional people who react based on their emotion. Their emotion comes to play first before their rationale. They will allow their pain to overshadow, cloud or override their good sense of judgement.

#35

Helpers serve by force, while Servants serve by choice

Romans 1:16

For I am not ashamed of the gospel of Christ, for it is the power of God to salvation for everyone who believes, for the Jew first and also for the Greek.

Romans 14:21-23

It is good neither to eat meat nor drink wine nor do anything by which your brother stumbles or is offended or is made weak. Do you have faith? Have it to yourself before God. Happy is he who does not condemn himself in what he approves. But he who doubts is condemned if he eats, because he does not eat from faith; for whatever is not from faith is sin.

Serving should not be a religious act. It should come naturally and not by force. It must be a matter of choice. The role of leaders these days is made more difficult by those who serve under them. Sometimes, it is more like you are forcing some stewards to serve. You have to persuade, cajole, sweet talk or promise them something before they serve. This shouldn't be the case.

Many of the saints we read about in the scripture were not forced to serve. They gave themselves to serving the Lord not being ashamed, but serving with conviction, integrity and truth. One of the greatest powers God gave man, is the power of volition, the power of choice. God never forces you to do what you don't want to do, except He wants to do it to His own glory. Serving God is a matter of choice and not by force. If you yield yourself to God as a vessel, He will use you, if you lift up your cup, He will fill it. He will not force you to lift up your cup, nor will He lift it up for you. You must make the effort and be willingly to serve Him.

Man has the history of forcing his fellow man to do things against their will. The slave trade in the 16th, 17th and 18th centuries is a typical example. So it is today with child soldiers and the human sex trade.

King Nebuchadnezzar, in Daniel chapter 3, forced a whole nation to worship the image he set up without giving anyone the opportunity to choose, but Shadrach, Meshach and Abednego had other ideas. When you force people to do anything against their will, you are taking their human rights away. God will not take anyone's rights away.

Helpers like this, are power drunk and take decisions irrationally without due process. They like to entice the people in the position of power and authority, by showing a different side of their idiosyncrasy that appears to be acceptable.

#36

Helpers take their eyes away off the ball, while Servants keep their eyes on the ball

Matthew 26:36-44

Then Jesus came with them to a place called Gethsemane, and said to the disciples, "Sit here while I go and pray over there." And He took with Him Peter and the two sons of Zebedee, and He began to be sorrowful and deeply distressed. Then He said to them, "My soul is exceedingly sorrowful, even to death. Stay here and watch with Me." He went a little farther and fell on His face, and prayed, saying, "O My Father, if it is possible, let this cup pass from Me; nevertheless, not as I will, but as You will." Then He came to the disciples and found them sleeping, and said to Peter, "What! Could you not watch with Me one hour? Watch and pray, lest you enter into temptation. The spirit indeed is willing, but the flesh is weak." Again, a second time, He went away and prayed, saying, "O My Father, if this cup cannot pass away from Me unless I drink it, Your will be done." And He came and found them asleep again, for their eyes were heavy. So He left them, went away again, and prayed the third time, saying the same words. Then He came to His disciples and said to them, "Are you still sleeping and

resting? Behold, the hour is at hand, and the Son of Man is being betrayed into the hands of sinners. Rise, let us be going. See, My betrayer is at hand."

Peter James and John, who were the three closest disciples to Jesus, could not 'watch' with Him, as the Bible says "even just for one hour". In Jesus' hour of need, they took their eyes off the ball. They fell asleep. Jesus told them of his sorrow and distress and gave them the simple task to watch with Him. But they failed Him. They couldn't fill the gap for Him. They couldn't sympathise or empathise with Him. They took their eyes off their assignment and allow their immediate needs to overshadow their commitment.

If you take your eyes off your calling or assignment, you allow complacency to creep in. You become weary and suffer from burn out. You lack foresight and become blind to your surroundings. Such people are weak and can't go the extra mile. They are never prepared and lack focus. They don't set goals or any parameter for their lives.

#37

Helpers stay in the valley, while Servants go to the mountain

Mark 6:46

And when he had sent them away, he departed into a mountain to pray.

Luke 5:16

But Jesus often withdrew to lonely places and prayed.

Matthew 14:23

After he had dismissed them, he went up on a mountainside by himself to pray. When evening came, he was there alone.

The dictionary meaning of a valley is "A low area of land between hills or mountains, typically with a river or stream flowing through it. A valley has two characteristics, one is low land, and another is being formed between hills or mountains. They are deep and narrow.

A valley of life is a comfort zone, it is a place of solitude where you are not in control of your situation. It is a place where your present and future are uncertain. It is a place where you are dependent on others for your existence. It is a crossroad of life, where you don't know what to do. A valley is a place of discouragements, disappointments, brokenness and frustrations. Everyone will one time or another go through the valley of life. But let's make no mistake, God is everywhere, He is omniscient and He is in the valley. This does not mean you have to stay there. David, in Psalm 23 in his darkest moment, described the valley as the shadow of death. But he was quick to emphasise, though it is the shadow of death, he is able to walk through it. **You can either stay in the valley and be washed away by the erosion of life, or you can go on the high mountain and take control of your life.**

You can either stay in the valley and be washed away by the erosion of life or go on the high mountain and take control of your life.

Let us go back to the meaning of a valley again. It is described as "A low area of land between hills or mountains, typically with a river or stream flowing through it." God's handy work is perfect. He knew a valley is not the best place to be in life, but he surrounded the valley with other things. The river, and the mountain. He is saying to us there is a way out of every valley we may find ourselves in. If you are in the valley, you must recognise that God is able to make a way. We must always bear in mind that His grace, and His mercy never fail and that they are more than sufficient.

The river that flows through a valley is full of life. The river is symbolic of a way out. God is saying it's not over yet, there is hope in the valley but you have to rely on Me. But He wants you to meet him on the mountain that is higher than you, because he doesn't want you to stay in the valley forever. He wants you to speak to your Pastor when you are going through difficulties, but not to rely on your Pastor and believe your problem will not go away until you've seen him. In other words, there is a part you have to play to overcome your valley experience; go to the mountain. It is not easy to reach the mountain particularly when you look at the mountain and it's so high up. So how do you go to the mountain? Firstly, by taking control of your situation through prayer, and supplication to God. Secondly, by recognising God can use anyone to trouble your trouble.

Jesus Christ is the supreme argument for prayer. When he was faced with the difficulty of laying down his life, he went up to the mountain to cry to His Father. He did not stay at the low land singing the song of defeat and disappointment.

Today's Pastors are becoming busier. They take up more responsibilities, travelling around the world to minister to their international audiences. Despite their national and international commitment, they still take time out to care for the sheep in the local church. It is therefore inevitable for such Pastors to handover a degree of the counselling to associate Pastors. I have witnessed stewards who refused to see an Associate Pastor and instead insist on seeing the "real Pastor." That is the spirit of a helper. That is staying in the valley.

There are other stewards or members, who are quite happy to receive counsel from any Pastor-on-Call, or seek the face of God directly. They know the God they serve is not only the God of their Pastor but a God in whom there is no partiality, variableness or shadow of turning. They know God for themselves and would rather go to the mountain and seek his face for divine intervention to their challenges. I am personally convinced that the reasons why the children of Israel often strayed away from God to follow other gods throughout the reign of many of the kings of Israel, was because they didn't know God for themselves. They only knew God as the God of Abraham not as their personal God. That is why Paul in his epistle to the ***Philippians in chapter 3:10 said; "That I may know him, and the power of his resurrection, and the fellowship of his sufferings, being made conformable unto his death;***

True servants know the Lord for themselves. They don't stay in the valley of their problems or challenges and wait for the church to call for fasting and prayer before they fast or pray. They have a personal relationship with God. They understand they have access to God as much as their Pastor. They are enrolled in the army of the Lord with the thorough knowledge of spiritual warfare. They are always dressed up for battle and are never caught unawares. They recognise the weapons of spiritual warfare are not carnal, but mighty through God.

Those who stay in the valley call a pity party around their trouble and sing the songs of sorrow and despair.

Those who stay in the valley are weaklings, they never aspire to eat meat but rather live like a baby, feeding on milk and sucking on the breast of others. They grow up physically but remain spiritually the same.

Those who stay in the valley call a pity party around their trouble and sing the songs of sorrow and despair. They always wear a long look with their countenance reminiscent of a phantom. They ignore their hygiene and forever look untidy. They dwell on the past, ignore the present and mortgage their future.

They hold on to the pain and kill themselves in instalments. They become repetitive telling the story of their problem over and over again until you are bored. Those who stay in the valley are attention seekers. They suck all day and sometimes lock themselves up refusing any help. They believe no one understands their situation and that the problem they are going through is unique to them alone because no one has ever gone through such a thing before. They are more likely to hop from one Church to the other seeking for solutions to their problem and in the process end up with more problems.

#38

Helpers see their position as their eternal right, while Servants see it as a privilege and opportunity

Matthew 2:1-5

Now after Jesus was born in Bethlehem of Judea in the days of Herod the king, behold, wise men from the East came to Jerusalem, saying, "Where is He who has been born King of the Jews? For we have seen His star in the East and have come to worship Him." When Herod the king heard this, he was troubled, and all Jerusalem with him. And when he had gathered all the chief priests and scribes of the people together, he inquired of them where the Christ was to be born. So they said to him, "In Bethlehem of Judea, for thus it is written by the prophet.

King Herod was the ruthless and callous King in Israel who tried to kill Jesus Christ. His family had ruled the kingdom and had built a dynasty over many years. It was therefore not a surprise that he believed it was his eternal right to rule. When he heard about the birth of Jesus; the King of the Jews, through the shepherds, he became so disturbed and sought to kill Him.

He saw Jesus as a potential rival who could one day be a threat to his kingdom. Herod would stop at nothing to protect his position and power. He even went to the extent of killing all children under the age of two in order to eliminate his "rival".

When we are in a position of power and authority we must see it as a privilege not as our right. Choosing lieutenants or leaders to lead an organisation or church is oftentimes the responsibility of the overall head, according to how he or she feels led by the Spirit. This task can be made more difficult when an incumbent leader takes offence when he or she is being replaced. A leader once took an offence to being replaced and left the church. In some cases it is more to do with those who are desperate to occupy a position and will scheme to get that position. If they don't get it they take a walk.

1 Samuel 16:5-13 (NKJV)

And he said, "Peaceably; I have come to sacrifice to the Lord. Sanctify yourselves, and come with me to the sacrifice." Then he consecrated Jesse and his sons, and invited them to the sacrifice. So it was, when they came, that he looked at Eliab and said, "Surely the Lord's anointed is before Him!" But the Lord said to Samuel, "Do not look at his appearance or at his physical stature, because I have refused him. For the Lord does not see as man sees; for man looks at the outward appearance, but the Lord looks at the heart." So Jesse called Abinadab, and made him pass before Samuel. And he said, "Neither has the Lord chosen this one." Then Jesse made Shammah pass by. And he said, "Neither has the Lord chosen this one." Thus Jesse made seven of his sons pass before Samuel. And Samuel said to Jesse, "The Lord has not chosen

these." And Samuel said to Jesse, "Are all the young men here?" Then he said, "There remains yet the youngest, and there he is, keeping the sheep." And Samuel said to Jesse, "Send and bring him. For we will not sit down till he comes here." So he sent and brought him in. Now he was ruddy, with bright eyes, and good-looking. And the Lord said, "Arise, anoint him; for this is the one!" Then Samuel took the horn of oil and anointed him in the midst of his brothers; and the Spirit of the Lord came upon David from that day forward. So Samuel arose and went to Ramah.

We also see in the scripture, the opposite attitude to King Herod. David was crowned the King of Israel, even when there was an incumbent King. David did not see his selection as his right to rule; he didn't immediately mount an assault on the incumbent King. Rather, it was the other way round. Saul was the one who sought to kill him. David knew that from the moment Samuel poured the oil on him that it was a great privilege and honour. He knew where he came from; a mere shepherd. He knew it had to be the grace of God for him to have been chosen above his brothers as he was the last born. He knew his father, or forefathers, had never ruled before and therefore his position was not his birth right.

Good servants see their position as an opportunity to help their generation.

David could have said to himself, "Here I am, I have arrived, I singlehandedly killed a lion and a bear, I killed the great Goliath, I am strong and young." He could have been carried away by the number of people who came to him at the Cave of Adullam. He refused to seize the moment of truth when Saul was exposed to him.

When people see their position as a right, as opposed to a privilege, they become a different person. They become brutal in the ways and manner they deal with their contemporaries. They don't mind stepping on other people's toes to achieve their aims. They are good pretenders and are always ready to wait for as long as it takes, while they skilfully plot their coup. They know how to win people to their side with their charming good manners and friendly attitude.

> ***They are conscious of why they are in the position, rather than why they shouldn't be in the position.***

Good servants see their position as an opportunity to help their generation. They see it as a chance to make a difference. They ask themselves questions such as "why me"? They are conscious of why they are in the position, rather than why they shouldn't be in the position.

#39

Helpers serve with self-rejection, while Servants serve with self-acceptance

Romans 14:22

Do you have faith? Have it to yourself before God. Happy is he who does not condemn himself in what he approves.

Luke 12:7

But even the very hairs of your head are all numbered. Fear not therefore: ye are of more value than many sparrows.

Psalm 139:13-18

For thou hast possessed my reins: thou hast covered me in my mother's womb. I will praise thee; for I am fearfully and wonderfully made: marvellous are thy serves; and that my soul knoweth right well. My substance was not hid from thee, when I was made in secret, and curiously wrought in the lowest parts of the earth. Thine eyes did see my substance, yet being unperfect; and in thy book all my members were written, which in continuance were fashioned, when as yet there was none of them. How precious also are thy thoughts unto me, O God! How great is the sum of them! If I should count them, they are more in number than the sand: when I awake, I am still with thee.

God did not create junk, neither did He create a reject. Pardon me to let my imagination loose for a minute. Psalm 139:14 talks about how man was fearfully and wonderfully made. Think about it for a second; the same God who in the twinkle of an eye created the heaven and earth and everything therein just by the pronouncement "Let there be", could have done the same with man. He wanted to come up with something special, something unique and exclusive. I believe he must have used the best material to make man. How then can we be so ungrateful to Him by rejecting what He spent quality time to create?

Nothing is more damaging to a healthy servant spirit than when we constantly reject ourselves. These kinds of stewards who reject themselves soon begin to reject others. They always try to outdo others. They often ask others how they are doing, become competitive and repetitive. You need to tip toe around them and carefully select your words in order not to offend them. They can turn goodwill gestures into bad ones. They become very snappy and very abrupt in their response to every sentence you make.

They complain when you show them love and complain when you don't. They feel they are unworthy to be loved and look to other people to meet a need or fill a vacuum only God can satisfy. They can't accept compliments. They reject themselves so much that when you tell them how nice their dress or shoes are; their response to you is "I only bought it for £5". You have not asked how much the dress or shoes cost, but because they don't think they are good enough to wear anything nice or expensive, they instantly put themselves down.

These kinds of stewards can have a negative effect on a team. The leader will spend quality time to spoon feed them and constantly supervise their work. When you give them a task, their first reaction is like that of the story of a boy once told by Pastor Matthew Ashimolowo. This young boy and his school mates, during the school lunch break set out to do a high jump. Every one of the boy's friends did their own jump but when it was his turn, he ran towards the bar and shook for a few minutes and turned back. This happened a number of times. His mates jumped until the bar was raised to the next level. The boy who had not done a single jump now complained. He wanted his friends to keep the bar on the same level, therefore preventing them from making progress.

A self-rejecting steward finds it difficult to have a social relationship with other people within their team. They build a spiritual wall around themselves for fear that if they let go and accept inward love, they will be rejected. You dare not ask them about their personal life otherwise they become frustrated and angry.

#40

Helpers serve with negative expectations, while Servants serve with positive expectations

Mark 10:46-52(NKJV)

Now they came to Jericho. As He went out of Jericho with His disciples and a great multitude, blind Bartimaeus, the son of Timaeus, sat by the road begging. And when he heard that it was Jesus of Nazareth, he began to cry out and say, "Jesus, Son of David, have mercy on me!" Then many warned him to be quiet; but he cried out all the more, "Son of David, have mercy on me!" So Jesus stood still and commanded him to be called. Then they called the blind man, saying to him, "Be of good cheer. Rise, He is calling you." And throwing aside his garment, he rose and came to Jesus. So Jesus answered and said to him, "What do you want Me to do for you?" The blind man said to Him, "Rabboni, that I may receive my sight." Then Jesus said to him, "Go your way; your faith has made you well." And immediately he received his sight and followed Jesus on the road.

Blind Bartimaeus, the beggar at the outskirts of Jericho heard that Jesus was passing. With his heart full of expectation, he shouted out, saying, "Jesus, Son of David, have mercy on me!" The more the people tried to shut him up and keep him quiet, the more he shouted until he received Jesus' attention. He was constant, resolute and dogged until his expectations were met. He was blind but at the end he could see.

True servants don't quit. They know exactly what they want and keep on asking until they get what they want. They recognise their needs and don't deny it, shy away from it, or try to explain it away. It is not that they believed Jesus owes them and must compensate them for serving Him; far from it. They know He is a just and good God, and able to do exceedingly and abundantly far beyond their imagination. They know God is true to His words and will always fulfil His promises.

The scripture makes God's desire for us so very clear in Jeremiah 29:11: that he has good thoughts towards us, not of evil, he wants to give us an expected end. In the knowledge of this, a true servant should be expectant not in arrogance but in humility.

Jonah 1-4(NKJV)

Now the word of the Lord came to Jonah the son of Amittai, saying, "Arise, go to Nineveh, that great city, and cry out against it; for their wickedness has come up before Me." But Jonah arose to flee to Tarshish from the presence of the Lord. He went down to Joppa, and found a ship going to Tarshish; so he paid the fare, and went down into it, to go with them to Tarshish from the presence of the Lord. But the Lord sent out a great wind on the sea, and there was a mighty tempest on the sea, so that the ship was about to be broken up. Then the mariners were afraid; and every man cried out to his god, and threw the cargo that was in the ship into the sea, to lighten the load. But Jonah had gone down into the lowest parts of the

ship, had lain down, and was fast asleep. So the captain came to him, and said to him, "What do you mean, sleeper? Arise, call on your God; perhaps your God will consider us, so that we may not perish." And they said to one another, "Come, let us cast lots that we may know for whose cause this trouble has come upon us." So they cast lots, and the lot fell on Jonah. Then they said to him, "Please tell us! For whose cause is this trouble upon us? What is your occupation? And where do you come from? What is your country? And of what people are you?" So he said to them, "I am a Hebrew; and I fear the Lord, the God of heaven, who made the sea and the dry land." Then the men were exceedingly afraid, and said to him, "Why have you done this?" For the men knew that he fled from the presence of the Lord, because he had told them. Then they said to him, "What shall we do to you that the sea may be calm for us?"—for the sea was growing more tempestuous. And he said to them, "Pick me up and throw me into the sea; then the sea will become calm for you. For I know that this great tempest is because of me."

Everyone travelling in the boat Jonah took when he tried to run away to Tarshish had no expectation. They were so afraid of the storm and believed they were going to die. When stewards serve without expectation, they cast away their faith. Notice what the Captain and the rest of the crew did. They became confused and lost. They threw away their food, prayed to different gods, cast lots and committed a serious crime of attempted murder. Such stewards are never focused and work without pattern and can't handle crises. They see their service only as a religious act that must be fulfilled.

#41

Helpers lack knowledge of the times, while Servants seek understanding of the times

1 Chronicles 12:32

And of the children of Issachar, which were men that had understanding of the times, to know what Israel ought to do; the heads of them were two hundred; and all their brethren were at their commandment. Then the king said to the wise men who understood the times (for this was the king's manner toward all who knew law and justice.

The Free Dictionary describes understanding as "The ability to learn, judge, make decisions." It also describes it as "having knowledge of, or familiarity with a particular thing".

The Oxford Dictionary described time as "The indefinite continued progress of existence and events in the past, present, and future regarded as a whole". It also describes time as the favourable or appropriate time to do something:

Carl Schultz in Baker's Evangelical Dictionary of Biblical Theology defined biblical understanding as; "To separate, to distinguish. "To have a perceptive insight with the ability to judge." To gain insight into something. He also likened it to the administrative functions of a king.

Now, let us marry the two words and its meaning together in line with 1 Chronicles 12:32. The children of Issachar are said to be men that had understanding of the times, and because of their understanding of the times, they knew what Israel ought to do. In other words, they have over the years possessed the ability to learn, judge, make decisions, familiarised themselves with the kingdom, have insight, and were aware of the appropriate time to do something. They had knowledge of administrative function of the kingdom. By so doing, they were able to create indefinite, continued progress of the kingdom, learning from the past, mastering the present and shaping the future.

Genesis 49:14-15

Issachar is a strong ass couching down between two burdens: and he saw that rest was good, and the land that it was pleasant; and bowed his shoulder to bear, and became a servant unto tribute.

A true servant must seek to have an Issachar anointing. What then is the Issachar anointing? We can only get the meaning from Genesis 49:14-15. Jacob called his 12 sons together to prophesy upon them before he passed away, and he described Issachar as a strong ass couching down between two burdens. Simply put, he was a man with a strong character, who bared on his shoulders the burdens of his brethren. He was a man ready to be stretched out in his service to God. Isaiah 9:6 shed more light on burden bearing and how the shoulder is the symbol of carrying burdens of others.

Isaiah 9:6

"For unto us a child is born, unto us a Son is given: and the government shall be upon His shoulder..."

A steward with the Issachar anointing must:

⇒ Be interested and able to give complete attention to the affairs and the administration of his or her ministry.

⇒ Have divine understanding and revelation knowledge of the ministry

⇒ Have good judgment and an ability to make good decision

⇒ Be diligent in his or her service

⇒ Have insight, foresight and far-sight

⇒ Be able to bring solution into difficult situations

⇒ Be able to discern and possess the ability to anticipate danger

⇒ Be dead to self and alive to God

⇒ Be ready to serve, yielding yourself to your calling, and not giving in to the pressures of life but focusing on God

A true servant must understand his or her organisation or ministry. He must understand the doctrine or core belief of the church. Why should Pastors be afraid to leave their church in the hands of their leaders for a few days, thinking their church could be in a mess by the time they return from a break or evangelical work? Many stewards lack real understanding of the times today. Have you asked yourself why Jesus spent so much time speaking in parables, even to His disciples? One would have thought they should have a good understanding of their Master given the time they have spent with Him.

When you lack understanding of the times, you are susceptible to errors and your judgments are impaired. You lack knowledge of what your organisation or church stands for. You stand for nothing and fall for everything. You are easily swept off your feet with heresy and deceit.

A young man once came to town with heresy, claiming his ministry could make everyone rich. He claimed every member would get a car within six months of joining the church. Many people rushed to his ministry including stewards. It wasn't long before they realised they had been "tangoed".

I heard of a steward who, because of his lack of understanding of the times, got angry. Angry because the leadership of the ministry refused to take his direction or do what he thought was necessary for the ministry to do. As good as his idea may have been, it was not the appropriate time to implement such idea. This steward became destructive, complained about everything, criticised the leadership of the ministry and eventually withdrew his stewardship.

#42

Helpers put family first, while Servants put God first

Luke 9:23-25

Then He said to them all, "If anyone desires to come after Me, let him deny himself, and take up his cross daily, and follow Me. For whoever desires to save his life will lose it, but whoever loses his life for My sake will save it. For what profit is it to a man if he gains the whole world, and is himself destroyed or lost?

1 Kings 19:20

Elisha then left his oxen and ran after Elijah. "Let me kiss my father and mother good-by," he said, "and then I will come with you." "Go back," Elijah replied. "What have I done to you?"

Matthew 8:18-22

And when Jesus saw great multitudes about Him, He gave a command to depart to the other side. Then a certain scribe came and said to Him, "Teacher, I will follow You wherever You go." And Jesus said to him, "Foxes have holes and birds of the air have nests, but the Son of Man has nowhere to lay His head." Then another of His disciples said to Him, "Lord, let me

first go and bury my father." But Jesus said to him, "Follow Me, and let the dead bury their own dead."

Luke 9:57-62

And it came to pass, that, as they went in the way, a certain man said unto him, Lord, I will follow thee whithersoever thou goest. And Jesus said unto him, Foxes have holes, and birds of the air have nests; but the Son of man hath not where to lay his head. And he said unto another, Follow me. But he said, Lord, suffer me first to go and bury my father. Jesus said unto him, let the dead bury their dead: but go thou and preach the kingdom of God. And another also said, Lord, I will follow thee; but let me first go bid them farewell, which are at home at my house. And Jesus said unto him, No man, having put his hand to the plough, and looking back, is fit for the kingdom of God.

Many of us have answered the call to serve without understanding what it is to say yes to God. We thought we can answer God and still hang on to our job, our family, our friends and business. We don't understand that serving God is about total commitment and sacrifice. It is yielding ourselves to His will, direction and instruction. It is being able to serve Him with all our heart and our strength. It's about self-denial. It's about not looking back, turning the care of our family to God and understanding that we cannot do it without His input. Many of us want position and power without commitment.

The scriptures above explained God's desire for us to be totally committed to Him and to our calling. Many of us will continuously use our children and work as an excuse to not attend an event or a meeting. We constantly call in to excuse ourselves from duty.

#42

Please understand that your work and your family are important and you must never ignore them.

> ***Many of us want position and power without commitment.***

Now let me get this straight out of the way. God is not saying we should forsake our family and concentrate on Him. He is not saying we should be married to Him as opposed to our spouse. He is simply saying we should get the balance and our priority right. He wants us to have quality time at home with our family and quantity time with Him. The majority of us never get it right.

Many of us did not go back to kiss our family 'goodbye' or kill our oxen as Elisha did. We do not carry our family along and make them understand our commitment to serving God.

Stewards who put God first have the opportunity to receive a double portion anointing just as Elisha:

⇒ They receive the assurance of God's covering over their family. Peter Mother-in-law was healed. Matthew 8:14-15

⇒ They never lack. The Levites received God's ordained sustenance through the required tithing of the nation. Numbers 18:21

⇒ They always receive God's backing and protection. The three Hebrew men were saved from the hands of King Nebuchadnezzar. Daniel 3:1-30

⇒ They experience God's miracle Elisha was fed by the selfish raven bird. 1 King 17:1-6

⇒ They experience God's remarkable promotion. Joseph was promoted to the position of Prime Minister. He rose from prison to palace. Genesis 41:1-46

#43

Helpers protect their own interest, while Servants protect the Kingdom's interest

Genesis 39:7-10

And it came to pass after these things that his master's wife cast longing eyes on Joseph, and she said, "Lie with me." But he refused and said to his master's wife, "Look, my master does not know what is with me in the house, and he has committed all that he has to my hand. There is no one greater in this house than I, nor has he kept back anything from me but you, because you are his wife. How then can I do this great wickedness, and sin against God?" So it was, as she spoke to Joseph day by day, that he did not heed her, to lie with her or to be with her.

Joseph was a slave in the household of Potiphar and could have easily succumbed to the constant seductions of his master's wife. After all, he was said to be alone with her in the room and no one would have known. He knew it was not only a sin against God but also against his master. He made up his mind to protect his master's interest as opposed to his own.

2 Samuel 4:4

Jonathan, Saul's son, had a son who was lame in his feet. He was five years old when the news about Saul and Jonathan came from Jezreel; and his nurse took him up and fled. And it happened, as she made haste to flee, that he fell and became lame. His name was Mephibosheth.

It is not unusual to see people focus on what someone had done wrong and not bother to look at what positives there are in the negatives. The scripture above said of the nurse of Jonathan's son, who, after the overthrow of King Saul and the death of Jonathan his employers, took little Mephibosheth and ran. In the attempt to save him from death, the boy fell, sustained serious injury and became lame. She could have picked herself up and run for her own life, after all the one who paid her salary was dead, but she chose to protect the interest of her master.

2 Samuel 13:1-18

And it came to pass after this, that Absalom the son of David had a fair sister, whose name was Tamar; and Amnon the son of David loved her. And Amnon was so vexed, that he fell sick for his sister Tamar; for she was a virgin; and Amnon thought it hard for him to do anything to her. But Amnon had a friend, whose name was Jonadab, the son of Shimeah David's brother: and Jonadab was a very subtil man. And he said unto him, Why art thou, being the king's son, lean from day to day? wilt thou not tell me? And Amnon said unto him, I love Tamar, my brother Absalom's sister. And Jonadab said unto him, Lay thee down on thy bed, and make thyself sick: and when thy father cometh to see thee, say unto him, I pray thee, let my sister Tamar come, and give me meat, and dress the meat in

my sight, that I may see it, and eat it at her hand. So Amnon lay down, and made himself sick: and when the king was come to see him, Amnon said unto the king, I pray thee, let Tamar my sister come, and make me a couple of cakes in my sight, that I may eat at her hand. Then David sent home to Tamar, saying, Go now to thy brother Amnon's house, and dress him meat. So Tamar went to her brother Amnon's house; and he was laid down. And she took flour, and kneaded it, and made cakes in his sight, and did bake the cakes. And she took a pan, and poured them out before him; but he refused to eat. And Amnon said, Have out all men from me. And they went out every man from him. And Amnon said unto Tamar, Bring the meat into the chamber that I may eat of thine hand. And Tamar took the cakes which she had made, and brought them into the chamber to Amnon her brother. And when she had brought them unto him to eat, he took hold of her, and said unto her, Come lie with me, my sister. And she answered him, Nay, my brother, do not force me; for no such thing ought to be done in Israel: do not thou this folly. And I, whither shall I cause my shame to go? And as for thee, thou shalt be as one of the fools in Israel. Now therefore, I pray thee, speak unto the king; for he will not withhold me from thee. Howbeit he would not hearken unto her voice: but, being stronger than she, forced her, and lay with her. Then Amnon hated her exceedingly; so that the hatred wherewith he hated her was greater than the love wherewith he had loved her. And Amnon said unto her, Arise, be gone. And she said unto him, there is no cause: this evil in sending me away is greater than the other that thou didst unto me. But he would not hearken unto

her. Then he called his servant that ministered unto him, and said, Put now this woman out from me, and bolt the door after her. And she had a garment of divers colours upon her: for with such robes were the king's daughters that were virgins apparelled. Then his servant brought her out, and bolted the door after her.

In the above scripture, Amnon took advantage of his own blood sister and raped her. The scripture said of him being sick because of his lust and his selfish interest. He would stop at nothing until he satisfied his interest and accomplished his mission of destruction. Stewards who put their interest above the ministry are naturally selfish and desperately wicked. They are insensitive, corny, charming and pretentious. They surround themselves with the wrong kind of people and seek advice from the haters of the ministry. They are users and name droppers. They present themselves as lovers of the ministry but they have a hidden agenda. They serve at their own convenience, and at the same time secretly gather members, using the resources of the ministry and holding unauthorised meetings. Their mission is to steal the sheep. Those they can't steal they betray, those they can't betray, they turn against.

#44

Helpers take advantage of their master's weakness, while Servants take advantage of their master's strength

2 Samuel 16:5-13

And when King David came to Bahurim, behold, thence came out a man of the family of the house of Saul, whose name was Shimei, the son of Gera: he came forth, and cursed still as he came. And he cast stones at David, and at all the servants of king David: and all the people and all the mighty men were on his right hand and on his left. And thus said Shimei when he cursed, Come out, come out, thou bloody man, and thou man of Belial: The Lord hath returned upon thee all the blood of the house of Saul, in whose stead thou hast reigned; and the Lord hath delivered the kingdom into the hand of Absalom thy son: and, behold, thou art taken in thy mischief, because thou art a bloody man. Then said Abishai the son of Zeruiah unto the king, Why should this dead dog curse my lord the king? let me go over, I pray thee, and take off his head. And the king said, What have I to do with you, ye sons of Zeruiah? so let him curse, because the Lord hath said unto him, Curse David. Who shall then say, Wherefore hast thou done so? And David said to Abishai, and to all his servants, Behold, my son, which came

forth of my bowels, seeketh my life: how much more now may this Benjamite do it? Let him alone, and let him curse; for the Lord hath bidden him. It may be that the Lord will look on mine affliction, and that the Lord will requite me good for his cursing this day. And as David and his men went by the way, Shimei went along on the hill's side over against him, and cursed as he went, and threw stones at him, and cast dust.

There is no perfect man on earth. Even the most powerful man has a moment of weakness. Leaders or Pastors can have challenges, either by their own making or by virtue of their position. Shimei took advantage of David's weak moment, he decided to throw stones at David and abused him. There is no doubt in my mind Shimei always harboured much hatred for David in his heart. He behaved out of the abundance of his heart. He must have looked forward to that moment and when it came, he seized the opportunity.

Ahithophel who was one of David's advisers and trusted allies, he also realised that David was getting weaker by the day and teamed up with Absalom to dethrone David (2 Samuel 15:31). Again in 1 Kings 1:1-7, Adonijah, who also was David's son, took advantage of his father's old age and declared himself king. Joab, who had for many years been David's joint Chief of Staff, and Abiathar the priest were quick to join the band wagon. Notice one thing that is common between both stories. The conspirators were all close people. Absalom and Adonijah were David's sons, his own flesh and blood. Ahithophel, Abiathar and Joab were three trusted men who wined and dined with David.

Stewards who behave like the four or five people described above are cowards. They are like snakes in the grass, full of venom looking for the right time to strike a victim unannounced.

1 Samuel 24:1-22 (NIV)

David Spares Saul's Life After Saul returned from pursuing the Philistines, he was told, "David is in the Desert of EnGedi." So Saul took three thousand able young men from all Israel and set out to look for David and his men near the Crags of the Wild Goats. He came to the sheep pens along the way; a cave was there, and Saulwent in to relieve himself. David and his men were far back in the cave. The men said, "This is the day the Lord spoke of when he said to you, 'I will give your enemy into your hands for you to deal with as you wish.'" Then David crept up unnoticed and cut off a corner of Saul's robe. Afterward, David was conscience-stricken for having cut off a corner of his robe. He said to his men, "The Lord forbid that I should do such a thing to my master, the Lord's anointed, or lay my hand on him; for he is the anointed of the Lord." With these words David sharply rebuked his men and did not allow them to attack Saul. And Saul left the cave and went his way. Then David went out of the cave and called out to Saul, "My lord the king!" When Saul looked behind him, David bowed down and prostrated himself with his face to the ground. He said to Saul, "Why do you listen when men say, 'David is bent on harming you'? This day you have seen with your own eyes how the Lord delivered you into my hands in the cave. Some urged me to kill you, but I spared you; I said, 'I will not lay my hand on my lord, because he is the Lord's anointed.' See, my father, look at this piece of your robe in my hand! I cut off the corner of your robe but did not kill you. See that there is nothing in my hand to indicate that I am guilty of wrongdoing

or rebellion. I have not wronged you, but you are hunting me down to take my life.

Let us look at David in the scripture above. He was in a position to kill Saul, who had been chasing and plotting to kill him. Rather, David refused to take advantage of his weakest moment, after all he was a man after his life. He knew he was the King of Israel, chosen and anointed by God. He understood he was God's representative. Haven't we seen or heard of Associate Pastors plotting against their boss in their weakest moments? You wouldn't have to search for long to find a church torn apart because of revolt by some Trustees or Leaders against the Pastor.

A true servant stands by their leader irrespective of their circumstance. They have a strong conscience and conviction. They have utmost respect and love for their leaders. They are submissive, and never dissuaded. They do not allow themselves to be influenced by friends, colleagues, or other mitigating factors.

#45

Helpers break ranks, while Servants close ranks

2 Samuel 15:19-22 (NIV)

The king said to Ittai the Gittite, "Why should you come along with us? Go back and stay with King Absalom. You are a foreigner, an exile from your homeland. You came only yesterday. And today shall I make you wander about with us, when I do not know where I am going? Go back, and take your people with you. May the Lord show you kindness and faithfulness." But Ittai replied to the king, "As surely as the Lord lives, and as my lord the king lives, wherever my lord the king may be, whether it means life or death, there will your servant be." David said to Ittai, "Go ahead, march on." So Ittai the Gittite marched on with all his men and the families that were with him.

To break ranks is to publicly show that you disagree with a group of which you are a member. It is to do or say something different from what the group you belong to does or says. To break ranks is to walk away from a straight row in which you and other soldiers have been standing. It is to fall out of line, particularly when under attack, or into disorder. It means failing to conform or to deviate.

In the scripture above, Ittai the Gittite, a foreigner who had only been with David for a short time, remained loyal to David despite the uncertainty. He pledged his allegiance even if it meant death. He was ready to risk his life for King David. This level of life and death faithfulness and loyalty is unparalleled. So also was Zadok, Abiathar and Amasa. They remained loyal to their leader, but Ahithophel, David's councillor betrayed him and teamed up with his son Absalom. He broke rank with his master.

Ittai the Gittite decided to put his Master first. He believed that David was the God-ordained monarch of Israel and he made up his mind to stick with him regardless of the circumstances. We must not forget that a majority of the people of Israel have decided to follow Absalom, including one or two of David's closest allies. They broke rank to team up with Absalom.

Jonathan is another example of a true servant. He refused to break rank with his friend David. His father King Saul was determined to eliminate David, but Jonathan refused to side with his father, despite the fact that Jonathan knew David would one day, replace his father as the King of Israel, and take his inheritance away from him. Jonathan was instrumental to the survival of David, even to the point of taking an oath with him (1 Samuel 19:1-17, 1 Samuel 20:1-17).

To close ranks on the other hand is to maintain order, discipline or solidarity. Those who close ranks are men and women of integrity; who understand authority and headship. They stick to you whatever the circumstance even unto death. They are genuine people who stand for the truth, even if it is against them. Their loyalty is more rooted in their belief, respect for authority and kind heart.

#45

Numbers 12:1-2

And Miriam and Aaron spake against Moses because of the Ethiopian woman whom he had married: for he had married an Ethiopian woman. And they said, Hath the Lord indeed spoken only by Moses? Hath he not spoken also by us? And the Lord heard it. Now the man Moses was very meek, above all the men which were upon the face of the earth.

The third verse of the scripture above described Moses as a meek man. He was a gentle and humble man chosen and ordained by God to deliver the children of Israel from slavery. Miriam and Aaron were his siblings; but they publicly disagreed with Moses' choice of wife and subsequently broke ranks with him. Today, there is no doubt that they would be labelled racist.

It would appear that these two people are really not concerned with Moses' choice of wife. I believe it is more to do with Moses' power, popularity and position. I believe they were jealous of him and only used his marriage as an opportunity to speak out. The second verse attests to this; ***"And they said, Hath the Lord indeed spoken only by Moses? Hath he not spoken also by us? And the Lord heard it."***

Stewards who break ranks usually lack finesse and diplomacy. They always struggle to manage their anger. They speak first and think later. They are never straight forward, very erratic and disorderly thereby making it difficult for you to figure out their motive. They look for the opportunity to entrap or outwit you. When you serve with people like this, you are never sure how to start a conversation with them. They always make you feel you are wrong.

#46

Helpers sit on the fence, while Servants sit on the roof top

Deuteronomy 5:1-9

And Moses called all Israel, and said unto them, Hear, O Israel, the statutes and judgments which I speak in your ears this day, that ye may learn them, and keep, and do them. The Lord our God made a covenant with us in Horeb. The Lord made not this covenant with our fathers, but with us, even us, who are all of us here alive this day. The Lord talked with you face to face in the mount out of the midst of the fire, (I stood between the Lord and you at that time, to shew you the word of the Lord: for ye were afraid by reason of the fire, and went not up into the mount;) saying, I am the Lord thy God, which brought thee out of the land of Egypt, from the house of bondage. Thou shalt have none other gods before me. Thou shalt not make thee any graven image, or any likeness of anything that is in heaven above, or that is in the earth beneath, or that is in the waters beneath the earth: Thou shalt not bow down thyself unto them, nor serve them: for I the Lord thy God am a jealous God, visiting the iniquity of the fathers upon the children unto the third and fourth generation of them that hate me.

To sit on the fence means that you can't decide what to do. You are torn between two choices, but cannot decide. You debate it in your head, but don't know what to do. When you sit on the fence you become unstable. Believe it or not, there are stewards who serve in one church this Sunday and in another the following Sunday. When you catch up with them they come up with all kinds of reasons.

Again there are stewards who serve and yet secretly slip away to some kind of program or event in town organised by individuals or organisations known for heresy and doctrines that are not in line with their local church and the fundamental teaching of the Bible. They run around town to satisfy their flesh, rather than satisfying the Lord. The scripture is clear and cannot be broken. You cannot serve two masters with the hope that you can have the 'best of both worlds.' You have to make up your mind where you want to be; here or there.

Matthew 6:24

No man can serve two masters: for either he will hate the one, and love the other; or else he will hold to the one, and despise the other. Ye cannot serve God and mammon."

A steward who sits on the fence lacks conviction in their beliefs and is more likely to change loyalties without any warning. In order to associate with a leader or a Pastor, they are ready to show their allegiance to two people, depending on who they are with at a given time. They are dishonest with themselves and others, and economical with managing the truth, as long as it is beneficial to them. They are filled with hypocrisy. When you sit on the fence your vision is impaired, you can only see around the vicinity of

True servants becomes the eyes of the organisation.

where you are. You become so short sighted that even when things happen around you, you don't know. You procrastinate, rather than do something, you do nothing.

Those who stand on the roof top, can see far away, you have a helicopter view of situations surrounding the organisation. You see danger before it comes. You are discerning in spirit. You are able to call the attention of your Leader or Pastor or the decision makers in your organisation.

In Bible times people stood on the walls of the city to check if the enemy was approaching. **True servants become the eyes of the organisation.**

#47

Helpers demand their master's inheritance, while Servants earn their masters inheritance

Elisha was not known as a great preacher or a great prophet when he was serving under Elijah. He was known only as a servant. Many people miss God's original purpose for their life because they look for fame in the ministry and not for the opportunity to serve the Lord or others. He patiently waited for his time to come, and it yielded great dividends for him. He eventually inherited a double portion of his master's anointing.

Luke 15:11-3(NKJV)

Then He said: "A certain man had two sons. And the younger of them said to his father, 'Father, give me the portion of goods that falls to me.' So he divided to them his livelihood. And not many days after, the younger son gathered all together, journeyed to a far country, and there wasted his possessions with prodigal living. But when he had spent all, there arose a severe famine in that land, and he began to be in want. Then he went and joined himself to a citizen of that country, and he sent him into his fields to feed swine. And he would gladly have filled his stomach with the pods that the swine ate, and no one gave him anything. "But when he came

to himself, he said, 'How many of my father's hired servants have bread enough and to spare, and I perish with hunger! I will arise and go to my father, and will say to him, "Father, I have sinned against heaven and before you, and I am no longer worthy to be called your son. Make me like one of your hired servants."'

I once heard of a church split into two because of an Associate Pastor who was determined to take over the leadership of the church. He undermined the Senior Pastor and managed to convince some members and leaders to support him in his selfish ambition to run the church. He eventually left the church with a majority of the members and leaders. The Pastor was so broken and almost gave up his calling. Little did he realise God was weeding out the 'dead wood' in the church. The church grew beyond the dreams of the Senior Pastor while the Associate Pastor, in a short period of time, lost a good number of the sheep he took with him.

A story was told of another church whose Senior Pastor was hounded, undermined and ridiculed by a handful of his leaders. His wife was constantly abused even in public places. There were times she was even prevented from entering her husband's office. At some point they took away the church car from the Pastor. The Pastor was led to move away from the denomination and establish his own independent ministry. The new ministry grew beyond measure and became the largest church not only in the city or country but in the entire continent. The Senior Pastor became renowned all over the world and became an opinion leader within the Christian and secular world. Today, he sits with Presidents,

Kings and business Leaders. He speaks around the world and is heavily sought after by the corporate and Christian world. We never heard of any of those leaders again.

Those who demand their master's inheritance are power conscious and will stop at nothing to achieve their selfish ends. They are abusive, vicious and manipulative. They lie about everything and present themselves as the 'messiah'. They gossip and spread rumours about their leaders and misrepresent them. They are parasites and gold diggers who will dig as deep as they can until they reach the gold.

#48

Helpers bury their talents, while Servants multiply their talents

Matthew 25:14-30

"For the kingdom of heaven is like a man traveling to a far country, who called his own servants and delivered his goods to them. And to one he gave five talents, to another two, and to another one, to each according to his own ability; and immediately he went on a journey. Then he who had received the five talents went and traded with them, and made another five talents. And likewise he who had received two gained two more also. But he who had received one went and dug in the ground, and hid his lord's money. After a long time the lord of those servants came and settled accounts with them. "So he who had received five talents came and brought five other talents, saying, 'Lord, you delivered to me five talents; look, I have gained five more talents besides them.' His lord said to him, 'Well done, good and faithful servant; you were faithful over a few things, I will make you ruler over many things. Enter into the joy of your lord.' He also who had received two talents came and said, 'Lord, you delivered to me two talents; look, I have gained two more talents besides them.' His lord

said to him, 'Well done, good and faithful servant; you have been faithful over a few things, I will make you ruler over many things. Enter into the joy of your lord.' "Then he who had received the one talent came and said, 'Lord, I knew you to be a hard man, reaping where you have not sown, and gathering where you have not scattered seed. And I was afraid, and went and hid your talent in the ground. Look, there you have what is yours.' "But his lord answered and said to him, 'You wicked and lazy servant, you knew that I reap where I have not sown, and gather where I have not scattered seed. So you ought to have deposited my money with the bankers, and at my coming I would have received back my own with interest. Therefore take the talent from him, and give it to him who has ten talents. 'For to everyone who has, more will be given, and he will have abundance; but from him who does not have, even what he has will be taken away. And cast the unprofitable servant into the outer darkness. There will be weeping and gnashing of teeth.'

Jesus told the story of three servants who were entrusted with treasures to invest. The first two invested the money given to them by their master and made profit. The third servant rather than invest, buried his talent and wasted it. Many stewards have great ideas and skills that may be beneficial to the church, but never put them to use because they don't want to give their all to the ministry. They let their talent waste away because they don't want anyone to know what they are good at. These people don't realise that they are burying their talents. If you don't put your God given talent to use, it remains dormant in you and will ultimately die.

#48

No wonder the richest part of the world is said to be the burial ground. It is full of millions of people who had great talents and either never used them to touch the world, or only used a tiny part of their gifts. **Good servants see their service to God as a spiritual act and sacrificial offering to God, a small way to say thank you for God's great love.**

Good servants see their service to God as a spiritual act and an offering to God, a small way to return the Father's great love.

#49

Helpers hold the dice, while Servants throw the dice

Matthew 14:22-33 (NKJV)

Immediately Jesus made His disciples get into the boat and go before Him to the other side, while He sent the multitudes away. And when He had sent the multitudes away, He went up on the mountain by Himself to pray. Now when evening came, He was alone there. But the boat was now in the middle of the sea, tossed by the waves, for the wind was contrary. Now in the fourth watch of the night Jesus went to them, walking on the sea. And when the disciples saw Him walking on the sea, they were troubled, saying, "It is a ghost!" And they cried out for fear. But immediately Jesus spoke to them, saying, "Be of good cheer! It is I; do not be afraid." And Peter answered Him and said, "Lord, if it is You, command me to come to You on the water." So He said, "Come." And when Peter had come down out of the boat, he walked on the water to go to Jesus. But when he saw that the wind was boisterous, he was afraid; and beginning to sink he cried out, saying, "Lord, save me!" And immediately Jesus stretched out His hand and caught him, and said to him, "O you of little faith, why did you doubt?"

And when they got into the boat, the wind ceased. Then those who were in the boat came and worshiped Him, saying, "Truly You are the Son of God."

Peter showed a remarkable desire to do the impossible. He was determined to learn from his Master and do what he saw him do. He was not phased, neither did he think for a second that he could not do the same thing as his Master. He threw the dice given to him by Jesus, while others decided to hold on to theirs. He took a step of faith by stepping into the water.

A Chinese proverb says "He that is afraid to shake the dice will never throw a six." How do you make progress if you hold on to your dice? Until you throw your dice you cannot make a difference.

Peter and the rest of the disciples saw Jesus walk towards them and were disturbed until they realised it was their Master. Peter however, did something remarkable. He immediately asked Jesus if he could come. He took the initiative by asking. Peter wouldn't by any chance make the attempt to take a walk without the Master. He asked first, knowing as long as the Master is there with him, he cannot fail. He wanted to learn from the Master, not learn the hard way.

He followed Jesus' instruction and started to do what he had never done before. However, as soon as the wind became more boisterous, Peter began to sink. He then cried out to the same person who taught him how to walk on water for help and immediately he got the help.

There are lessons to learn from the scripture.

⇒ **He asked Jesus if he could come**

Sometimes you come across stewards who jump to carry out a task without any instruction because of jealousy or burning desire to do like others do. They are too impatient to go through the learning process and end up jumping the gun.

If you are to take the initiative, you must do it with the right spirit. Not for your own self-promotion, but for the benefit of the department, or the organisation.

⇒ **He followed Jesus' instruction to come. Peter did as Jesus had commanded**

Peter realised taking an initiative does not necessarily mean he is now above instruction. He understood that he was a man under instruction and the authority of his Mentor and Master.

When you throw your dice or take an initiative, you have to do it within the rules and guidelines of your organisation. There must be a line you know you cannot cross.

⇒ **When he ran into trouble he called out for help from the person who gave the instruction.**

One thing is to make a mistake, which is acceptable, the worst thing is to either try to fix it without seeking for the right help or try to cover it up.

Taking an initiative is taking a risk in the first instance and surely there is every possibility of mistakes being made in the process. We must understand that without committing our initiatives to God, mistakes are inevitable. The moment you think you can make it happen by yourself and don't need God, your leaders or your Pastor, you already determine where your initiative will end.

Proverbs 16:33 (NLT)

We may throw the dice, but the Lord determines how they fall.

Peter was ready to do what he had never done before. He was ready to learn from the person who had the knowledge. Some stewards sometimes think they are better or more knowledgeable than others. They are not ready to learn from those more experienced within the department. They want to swim across, throwing themselves at the very deep end of the river and end up sinking.

When you throw the dice You are adding value to the department or organisation

Peter shouted out for help rather than try to fix the problem himself. He relied on his dependable Master to assist him when he ran into trouble. He did not try to prove how smart or intelligent he was. He asked for help

When you throw the dice:

⇒You are adding value to the department or organisation

⇒You are releasing the potential inside of you

⇒You are building and positioning yourself for God's promotion

⇒You can see and acknowledge problems and then focus on finding solutions and opportunities

⇒You are objective and are disciplined in your approach to your task

Other disciples stayed in the boat because they were scared. They held on to their dice. They watched Peter as he made a difference. When Peter began to sink, I guess one of them must have said something like; “Ah! I knew it! Peter, Peter, he thinks he is smart. Who does he think he is anyway?”

Stewards who hold on to their dice see challenges and do nothing about it. They magnify a problem rather than make an attempt to solve it. They will always wait for someone else to make a move or call the attention of others. They ignore tasks or dance around them without making a difference.

#50

Helpers obey but with a wrong attitude, while Servants obey but with a right attitude

Judges 5:2

Praise ye the LORD for the avenging of Israel, when the people willingly offered themselves.

1 Chronicles 28:9

And thou, Solomon my son, know thou the God of thy father, and serve him with a perfect heart and with a willing mind: for the LORD searcheth all hearts, and understandeth all the imaginations of the thoughts: if thou seek him, he will be found of thee; but if thou forsake him, he will cast thee off forever.

Isaiah 1:19

If ye be willing and obedient, ye shall eat the good of the land:

Taking direction from your leader does not necessarily mean you are submissive. Your attitude and actions determine whether you are willing or not. If you carry out the task grudgingly God sees your heart, even if your leader or your Pastor don't see it. You must serve with a perfect heart and a willing mind. Submission should be unconditional. When you are given a task and you accept the task only because you don't have a choice. You are a steward with a wrong attitude. If you grumble or complain about the task, you are a steward with a wrong attitude. When you accept a task, you must accept it willingly and with a perfect heart. The scripture in

1 Chronicles 28:9 is clear. ***"The Lord searcheth all hearts and understandeth all imagination of the thoughts" God sees all and knows all.***

Only when you are willing does your obedience become complete. Then you are able to receive the reward. Isaiah 1:19 attests to this. In other words, your willingness to take up responsibilities in your department determines the level of your reward.

When your attitude to your work or service to God is wrong, you will end up with a mediocre result. Your work will be punctuated with errors which could bring embarrassment to the organisation. When your attitude is wrong, the quality of you work doesn't matter to your colleagues. Your work will not be valued by them because you attach little importance to it. Stewards with the wrong attitude are full of venom, always angry and they are frustrated. They create an unpleasant atmosphere within the team or department. They harm others with their attitude, and make people feel bad and unhappy. **The wrong attitude produces negative effects. It lowers the overall morale and productivity in the department. It has the tendency to spread among others, causing team members to become apathetic and dejected.** Stewards with a wrong attitude are often lazy, tardy and rude. They find it difficult to collaborate with others and this affects how they contribute to the progress of their organisation.

#51

Helpers justify their wrongs, while Servants acknowledge their wrongs

Luke 10:25-29

And, behold, a certain lawyer stood up, and tempted him, saying, Master, what shall I do to inherit eternal life? He said unto him, What is written in the law? How readest thou? And he answering said, Thou shalt love the Lord thy God with all thy heart, and with all thy soul, and with all thy strength, and with all thy mind; and thy neighbour as thyself. And he said unto him, Thou hast answered right: this do, and thou shalt live. But he, willing to justify himself, said unto Jesus, And who is my neighbour?

Genesis 3:9-13

And the Lord God called unto Adam, and said unto him, where art thou? And he said, I heard thy voice in the garden, and I was afraid, because I was naked; and I hid myself. And he said, who told thee that thou wast naked? Hast thou eaten of the tree, whereof I commanded thee that thou shouldest not eat? And the man said, the woman whom thou gavest to be with me, she gave me of the tree, and I did eat. And the Lord God said unto the woman, what is this that thou hast done? And the woman said, the serpent beguiled me, and I did eat.

Man has perfected the act of self-justification because we always want to be right and look right. When children have done something wrong and they are asked the question, "What happened? How often have you heard the following phrases "It wasn't me", "I didn't do it!" or, "It's not my fault!" Have you come across stewards when things goes wrong, who will come up with phrases like; "That's not my responsibility" or, "That's not my job!" or " don't know about it" or "Ask Brother A about it""

The blame game started from Adam and Eve. We all have the tendency to justify ourselves to other people just as Adam and Eve did, even when we know we are wrong. God asked Adam a simple question ***"Hast thou eaten of the tree, whereof I commanded thee that thou shouldest not eat"? Genesis 3:11.*** What was Adam's response? Rather than own up to his crime and his inability to manage his home, he told God it was his wife's fault. He said to God; ***"the woman whom thou gavest to be with me, she gave me of the tree, and I did eat." (Genesis 3:12).*** His wife did the same thing when God asked her a similar question; she turned around and blamed the serpent.

King Saul did a similar thing in 1 Samuel 151-35. God told Samuel, the prophet, to go and tell King Saul to put his army together and go out to battle against the Amalekites who fought against Moses and the Israelites when they came out of Egypt. He commanded Saul not to spare any life be it oxen, sheep or camels. Saul did as he was told but for one or two things; he spared the life of the King of Amalekites and he and his soldiers brought back the best of the land to Israel. God then sent Samuel back to Saul to confront him with his action of disobedience. Rather than own up to his sin, Saul tried to justify it (1 Samuel 15:18-21). Again in Luke 10:25-29, a lawyer tried to justify his righteousness.

A true servant serves in humility. They are modest in their behaviour and submissive in their attitude. They are non-judgmental and are quick to repent. They are considerate and never try to take credit for anything they do on behalf of the department. They have a teachable spirit. They listen and pay more attention to instruction. They recognise they may not the best at everything and therefore appreciate the talents and qualities of others. Without humility, it is always going to be difficult to accept our wrongs. When we try to justify ourselves, we are saying we are infallible. We give excuses for our mistakes rather than own up to them. We strive at all times to validate what is wrong. Even when it is obvious we are wrong, we come up with reasons to justify the wrongs.

When we try to justify, we are saying we are above correction and always on the defensive. Such people can't accept positive feedback; they believe feedback is an attack on their person.

#52

Helpers throw a spanner at other people's ideas and suggestions, while Servants use a spanner on other people's

Nehemiah 4:1-5 (NKJV)

But it so happened, when Sanballat heard that we were rebuilding the wall, that he was furious and very indignant, and mocked the Jews. And he spoke before his brethren and the army of Samaria, and said, "What are these feeble Jews doing? Will they fortify themselves? Will they offer sacrifices? Will they complete it in a day? Will they revive the stones from the heaps of rubbish—stones that are burned?" Now Tobiah the Ammonite was beside him, and he said, "Whatever they build, if even a fox goes up on it, he will break down their stone wall." Hear, O our God, for we are despised; turn their reproach on their own heads, and give them as plunder to a land of captivity! Do not cover their iniquity, and do not let their sin be blotted out from before You; for they have provoked You to anger before the builders.

There are people like the two men mentioned above in the world today. People who are not ready to do the job but will do everything to stop others. People, who hang around the department, make noise, and eat and drink without contributing anything. Their main tasks are to look for faults in what others do.

Nehemiah came up with a good and constructive idea to rebuild the wall that was damaged over several years. Because of this, Sanballat and Tobiah became so envious and angry of Nehemiah and the Jews. They ridiculed them and poured scorn on their efforts to rebuild the wall. They did everything to stop the wall from being built. These two men even tried to lure Nehemiah to a secluded plain called Ono with the aim of harming him. They were persistent in their attempt to distract and dissuade Nehemiah.

Stewards who throw spanners constantly try to capture the minds of people and play on their emotions, with the ultimate aim of suffocating and killing the idea in its infancy.

Stewards who throw spanners constantly try to capture the minds of people and play on their emotions, with the ultimate aim of suffocating and killing the idea in its infancy. They use fear, depression, mockery and doubts to demoralise people. They are never happy when others come up with ideas and will do everything to kill the idea. They throw the spanners in an attempt to discredit the originator of the idea. They hinder the service of God by doing nothing. They are stubborn, rebellious, and resistant to the truth.

Servants embrace other people's idea and offer to serve with the person irrespective of who he or she may be. They buy into the idea and run with it. They focus more on the idea's positives than its negatives.

#53

Helpers hold on to their father's culture and traditions, while Servants adopt the kingdom culture and traditions

Mark 7:9

He said to them, "All too well you reject the commandment of God, that you may keep your tradition.

Matthew 15:3

He answered and said to them, "Why do you also transgress the commandment of God because of your tradition?

Luke 16:13 (NIV)

"No one can serve two masters. Either you will hate the one and love the other, or you will be devoted to the one and despise the other. You cannot serve both God and money."

Globalisation and immigration have undoubtedly had a positive effect on the sociological, cultural and demographical makeup of the church today. This does mean churches have to adjust in order to accommodate people with different cultures and languages. It is very common today to find up to ten or more cultures and languages represented in a local church. It is therefore not practical to adopt all the languages represented in the church, thus the need to adopt just one language. A servant will embrace and abide by the language, while a helper will rather stick to his or her language.

Let us look at it from another angle. A few years ago, a young lady steward in my local church lost her dad and according to her tradition and culture, she was supposed to shave her head and stay in doors for a period of days to honour her dad and appease the gods of their ancestors. This obviously is not in line with her faith. She refused because she would rather do the will of God, than satisfy her culture. She was threatened with being ostracised.

A Kingdom culture conscious steward respects others. They see others as part of a big family of God. They recognise they are firstly a citizen of the kingdom before they are citizen of whichever country they may have come from.

This is not an attempt to rid you of your culture or tradition. It is to ensure they are in line with Kingdom culture. If your culture clashes with that of the Kingdom, then there is only one thing to choose; the Kingdom culture. We see how the culture of man has found its way into the church, reflecting on how the church is run. Some churches are so mono-cultural in there set up that you can smell it from afar.

Kingdom culture conscious steward respects others. They see others as part of the big family of God. They recognise they are firstly a citizen of the kingdom before they are citizen of whichever country they may have come from. They treat everyone the same way.

When you hold on to your culture and tradition, you believe they are paramount and above the culture of the Kingdom of God. You become unstable and unpredictable. You cause division and create fear among others. You blow hot and cold and you are not really sure which way to go.

#54

Helpers are laggards, while Servants are pace setters

1 Samuel 30:8-10

And David enquired at the Lord, saying, Shall I pursue after this troop? shall I overtake them? And he answered him, Pursue: for thou shalt surely overtake them, and without fail recover all. So David went, he and the six hundred men that were with him, and came to the brook Besor, where those that were left behind stayed. But David pursued, he and four hundred men: for two hundred abode behind, which were so faint that they could not go over the brook Besor.

The word laggard is defined in the English dictionary as follows: To fail to keep up a pace; straggle, to proceed or develop with comparative slowness, to fail, weaken, or slacken gradually; a condition of slowness or retardation.

Servants serve by example and lead from the front. In Bible times it is common to see Kings go to battle with their soldiers. They are at the very forefront of every battle and risk their lives. They don't see themselves as either too big or too important to go to war. They lead from the front and live or die by their actions.

The enemy invaded Ziklag and took the wives, sons and daughters of the inhabitant's captive. After King David had inquired of the Lord, he personally led the army to pursue the rebels and took back all they had taken away. David knew that as the head, the buck stopped with him. He understood that the overall responsibility lay at his feet. He was spontaneous in his reaction to the problem. He knew going out with the army to battle would at the least motivate and galvanise his army. On one occasion David stayed at home, rather than go to war, we know what happened to him; he ended up sleeping with another man's wife. Everything that could possibly go wrong, will go wrong when you shift your responsibilities to others.

2 Samuel 11:1-5

And it came to pass, after the year was expired, at the time when kings go forth to battle, that David sent Joab, and his servants with him, and all Israel; and they destroyed the children of Ammon, and besieged Rabbah. But David tarried still at Jerusalem. And it came to pass in an evening tide, that David arose from off his bed, and walked upon the roof of the king's house: and from the roof he saw a woman washing herself; and the woman was very beautiful to look upon. And David sent and enquired after the woman. And one said, Is not this Bathsheba, the daughter of Eliam, the wife of Uriah the Hittite? And David sent messengers, and took her; and she came in unto him, and he lay with her; for she was purified from her uncleanness: and she returned unto her house. And the woman conceived, and sent and told David, and said, I am with child.

I often tell Leaders serving with me how they need to lead from the front and not from the comfort of their home. You don't stay at home and dish out instructions to other stewards, only to come back and blame them if there are any mistake. While delegation is an integral and fundamental management principle, it does not however mean delegating and detaching yourself. You have to remain constant and be a part of the overall process from start to finish.

Laggard stewards fail to keep up the pace. They are slack in their approach and slow to react to important issues. They are never at the forefront of implementing tasks. It does not matter how long they have been born again, their mind still remains unrenewed. They remain untransformed and struggle with the same sin they used to commit long ago.

#55

Helpers are stress masters, while Servants are stretch masters

Genesis 13:5-11

Now Lot, who was moving about with Abram, also had flocks and herds and tents. But the land could not support them while they stayed together, for their possessions were so great that they were not able to stay together. And quarreling arose between Abram's herders and Lot's. The Canaanites and Perizzites were also living in the land at that time. So Abram said to Lot, "Let's not have any quarreling between you and me, or between your herders and mine, for we are close relatives. Is not the whole land before you? Let's part company. If you go to the left, I'll go to the right; if you go to the right, I'll go to the left." Lot looked around and saw that the whole plain of the Jordan toward Zoar was well watered, like the garden of the Lord, like the land of Egypt. (This was before the Lord destroyed Sodom and Gomorrah.) So Lot chose for himself the whole plain of the Jordan and set out toward the east. The two men parted company.

Lot was Abraham's nephew. His father Haram died when he was young and Abraham took over the responsibility of Lot's father.

God spoke to Abraham in Genesis 12:1 to leave his father's house to go to another city where he promised to prosper him. Abraham took Lot his nephew with him. Little did he realise his nephew was going to give him so much stress and grief. Lot gave his uncle Abraham lots of trouble and became an albatross around his neck.

Firstly, Lot allowed his servants to quarrel with his Uncle's servants. It took Abraham to intercede to create some sort of order. He asked that they separate, each going in the opposite direction.

Secondly, Lot disrespected Abraham by choosing the new land first, not allowing his Uncle to choose first. He chose Sodom and Gormorrah where he was eventually taken captive when the city was invaded by the enemy (Genesis 14:16). Abraham had to take his servants and went after the captors to rescue his nephew.

Lot was so carried away by what his physical eyes could see. The scripture says he looked around and saw that the plain of Jordan towards Zoar was well watered. He made his decision based on the external appearance of the plain. He saw the beauty of the plain, adorned with roses. What he failed to recognise were the thorns on the lovely roses. The extremely wicked cities of Sodom and Gomorrah were situated there and pretty soon his lust towards the temporary and perishable things soon caught up with him. Lot took advantage of his Uncle's generosity to choose first. In the culture he grew up in, it was customary for the older person to choose before the younger. One would have thought that out of respect to his uncle, Lot would have returned the

If you are a steward or an associate Pastor, and your leader or Pastor is not at peace with you. If he is always worried about your next action, or he is unable to leave the church in your hands, you are a stress master.

generosity. He saw the generosity as an advantage or edge, over his Uncle. Thirdly, Abraham had to intercede for Lot with God. God was going to destroy the city of Sodom where Lot lived, because of her sins. He had to send in Angels to rescue Lot and his family. What a nephew from hell.

If you are a steward or an Associate Pastor, and your leader or Pastor is not at peace with you. If he is always worried about your next action, or he is unable to leave the church in your hands, you are a stress master.

Stress masters are easy believers, always wanting the easy task. They take you for granted and always take advantage of your generosity. They want to walk before they can crawl. They tend not to learn from their mistakes. They make the same mistakes over and over again and blame others for their folly. They cannot be counted upon once they are away from the gaze of their Pastor or their Leader. They become spiritually unstable and are easily moved by what they see. They are led by their sight and always lust towards the mundane things of this world. They make decisions based on external appearances. They always believe the grass is greener on the other side. They don't understand that not all that glitters is gold. A stressful steward is like a parasite. They hang around you and suck you dry until you have nothing else to give. They live off you, obtaining nourishment and protection while offering no benefit in return. They belch in your face and never offer help. They are human parasites; often harmful to the body and cause disease.

Hebrews 3:12-13 encourages believers to exhort one another daily. In other words to encourage each other, to stretch each other and not to stress each other.

1 Samuel 23:15–18

And David abode in the wilderness in strong holds, and remained in a mountain in the wilderness of Ziph. And Saul sought him every day, but God delivered him not into his hand. And David saw that Saul was come out to seek his life: and David was in the wilderness of Ziph in a wood. And Jonathan Saul's son arose, and went to David into the wood, and strengthened his hand in God. And he said unto him, Fear not: for the hand of Saul my father shall not find thee; and thou shalt be king over Israel, and I shall be next unto thee; and that also Saul my father knoweth. And they two made a covenant before the Lord: and David abode in the wood, and Jonathan went to his house.

Let us examine the text above. Saul sought to kill David because he was set aside to take over his kingdom but Saul was not having it. He sought after him every day and night. David had no choice but to hide in the wilderness. It took Jonathan, Saul's son to come to the aid of David. Jonathan not only helped David to escape the wrath and the fury of his wicked father, he also helped David to hold fast to the promises of God. Verse 16 says "And Jonathan Saul's son arose, and went to David into the wood, and strengthened his hand in God".

Jonathan knew David was in a very difficult situation. He realised he would be at his lowest ebb, weak and in despair. He sought after David to strengthen his hand in the Lord. He sought after him to exhort and encourage him to put on the whole armour of God. He stretched his faith by reminding him of God's promises and purpose for his life. He pointed David to Jesus Christ for hope and strength and helped him to build his self-confidence. Notice what verse 17 says: ***"And he said unto him, Fear not: for the hand of Saul my father shall not find thee; and thou shalt be king over Israel, and I shall be next unto thee; and that also Saul my father knoweth."***

Servants make sentient effort to strengthen the hands of their brother or sister. They stretch your faith not only by what they say but also by what they do. When you are about to give up, a true servant will remind you of the Promises and the covenant of God. They point you in the right direction and stand with you until you win. They not only stretch your faith, they also help you to build your hope in the time when nothing seems to work.

They stretch your faith not only by what they say but also by what they do.

86492534R00120

Made in the USA
Columbia, SC
14 January 2018